TOP 10
CRETE

DK

EYEWITNESS TRAVEL

Left **Dolphin fresco, Knosos** Right **Rethymno harbour**

LONDON, NEW YORK,
MELBOURNE, MUNICH AND DELHI
www.dk.com

Produced by Blue Island Publishing
Reproduced by Colourscan, Singapore
Printed and bound in China by Leo Paper
Products Ltd

First published in Great Britain in 2003 by
Dorling Kindersley Limited
80 Strand, London WC2R 0RL A Penguin
Company

**Copyright 2003, 2009 ©
Dorling Kindersley Limited,
London**

Reprinted with revisions 2005, 2007, 2009

A CIP catalogue record is available from the
British Library.

ISBN 978-1-40533-350-4

Within each Top 10 list in this book, no
hierarchy of quality or popularity is implied.
All 10 are, in the editor's opinion, of roughly
equal merit.

Contents

Crete's Top 10

Ancient Knosos	8
Irakleio	12
Irakleio Archaeological Museum	14
Chania	18
Phaestos	20
Rethymno	22
Gortys	24
Samaria Gorge	26
The Amari Valley and Mt Idi	28
Gournia	30
Moments in History	32
Ancient Sites	34
Art and Archaeological Museums	36
Folklore Museums	38
Venetian and Turkish Castles	40
Churches and Monasteries	42
Beach Resorts	44
Islands and Boat Trips	46

Front – **DK Images:** Robin Gauldie bl; **Superstock**: age fotostock main. Back – **DK Images**: Nigel Hicks tc, tr;
Robin Gauldie tl. Spine – **DK Images**: Peter Jousiffe b.

Key to abbreviations
Adm *admission charge payable* **Free** *no admission charge*

Left **Plakias** Right **Tavernas, Chersonisos**

Villages	48
Areas of Natural Beauty	50
Mountain Walks	52
Wildlife	54
Famous Cretans	56
Myths and Legends	58
Music and Instruments	60
Festivals and Events	62
Markets and Shopping Streets	64
Food and Drink	66
Restaurants	68
Tavernas	70
Cafés and Ouzeries	72
Nightlife	74

Around the Island

Central Crete	78
Western Crete	90
Eastern Crete	102

Streetsmart

Getting To and Around Crete	116
General Information	117
Things to Avoid	118
Special Interest Holidays	119
Eating and Drinking Tips	120
Shopping Tips	121
Budget Ideas	122
Families and Disabled Visitors	123
Banking and Communications	124
Health and Security Tips	125
Places to Stay	126
General Index	132

Left **Castle, Paleochora** Right **Siteia harbour**

Following pages **Siteia beach**

CRETE'S TOP 10

Highlights of Crete
6–7

Ancient Knosos
8–11

Irakleio
12–13

Irakleio Archaeological
Museum
14–15

Chania
18–19

Phaestos
20–21

Rethymno
22–23

Gortys
24–25

Samaria Gorge
26–27

The Amari Valley
and Mt Idi
28–29

Gournia
30–31

Top 10 of Everything
32–75

CRETE'S TOP 10

ᴛᴏᴘ 10 Highlights of Crete

Although it could not be more Greek, Crete is really a country within a country, with its own history, folklore and traditions. It was the birthplace of Europe's oldest civilization, the enigmatic Minoan culture which flourished over 4,000 years ago. Greeks, Romans, Byzantines, Saracens, Venetians and Turks also left their mark. This rich human heritage is set against the backdrop of magnificent mountain scenery and beaches lapped by a deep blue sea.

Irakleio
A good place to see a slice of everyday Greek street life, Crete's capital is an eclectic mix of medieval Venetian fortifications, bustling markets and modern streets *(see pp12–13).*

Ancient Knosos
Knosos is among the most impressive relics of the ancient Mediterranean world. The Minoan palace was imaginatively reconstructed in the early 20th century *(see pp8–11).*

Irakleio Archaeological Museum
Crete's leading museum houses amazing finds from Knosos and other great archaeological sites *(see pp14–15).*

Chania
Once the island's capital, this pretty little harbour town, with good beaches nearby and lots of open-air restaurants and shops, makes a great base for exploring Crete's wild west *(see pp18–19).*

Phaestos
One of the most important Minoan palace sites in Crete, Phaestos is a fascinating maze of walls, stairways and courtyards on a hillside overlooking the Messara plain and the Libyan Sea *(see pp20–21).*

Rethymno
6 Crete's third largest city is packed with reminders of a multi-layered history. A huge castle, Turkish mosques, Venetian town houses and bustling markets are part of the charm, along with a beach esplanade (see pp22–3).

Gortys
7 The bases of toppled Roman columns, the ruins of a Byzantine basilica, post-Minoan fortifications, an agora, acropolis and remains of temples to Athena and Apollo all hint at the chequered past of Gortys (see pp24–5).

Samaria Gorge
8 The "White Mountains" of the Sfakia region dominate southwest Crete. This rugged massif, most of which can only be explored on foot, as there are few roads, is cloaked in pine trees and traversed by the lovely Samaria Gorge (see pp26–7).

Fodele • Irakleio **2 3** Limin Chersonisos · Sea of Crete
Malia
ageia · Kasteli **1** Knosos
Neapolis
Varvari Kritsa · Agios Nikolaos · Skopi · Siteia · Vai
IRAKLEIO Oros Dikti Gournia **10**
7 Gortys Ano Viannos LASITHI Zakros
Agioi Deka Makrygialos
Ierapetra
Mediterranean Sea

The Amari Valley & Mt Idi
9 Old-fashioned villages, empty mountain panoramas and legend-laden caves seem like part of a different world, and can easily be explored with a rented car or escorted coach tour (see pp28–9).

Gournia
10 The best preserved Minoan town on Crete has a honeycomb-like labyrinth of tiny houses and narrow lanes surrounding a small palace overlooking the Gulf of Mirabello (see pp30–31).

🔟 Ancient Knosos

Knosos is steeped in mystery and enchantment. In legend, it was the seat of King Minos, beneath whose palace the bull-headed Minotaur hunted its victims in the labyrinth built by Daedalus. In reality, it was the hub of a Bronze Age empire that held sway over the Aegean more than 4,000 years ago. This part of the Knosos story only began to be unearthed at the beginning of the 20th century, when British archaeologist Sir Arthur Evans began excavations of the site.

Dolphin Frescoes

The queen's rooms were lavishly decorated with frescoes of leaping dolphins and well equipped with a bath and even a flush lavatory.

Central court

⏱ If possible, visit Knosos in spring or autumn, when cooler weather makes exploring more pleasant than in high summer. But if you are holidaying in peak season, get to the site as soon as it opens, before most coach tour groups have arrived.

🍴 There are several tavernas and snack bars within a few steps of the site entrance, along the main road to Irakleio.

• Map K4 • Route 97, 5 km (8 miles) south of Irakleio • 2810 231940
• Summer: 8am–7pm daily; winter: 8:30am–3pm daily • Closed some national holidays
• Adm €6; concessions €3; combined ticket for Knosos and Irakleio Archaeological Museum (see pp14–15) available
• Disabled access difficult

Top 10 Sights

1. Central Court
2. Piano Nobile
3. Dolphin Frescoes
4. Storehouses
5. South Portico
6. Great Staircase
7. Hall of Double Axes
8. North Entrance Passage
9. Throne Room
10. Bust of Sir Arthur Evans

Central Court

All Minoan palaces were built around a central courtyard. This would have been the hub of the complex and would probably have been used for ceremonial purposes and for royal audiences. The courtyard of Knosos has a commanding view of the valley.

Piano Nobile

Evans dubbed this expansive room on the upper floor of the palace building the "noble hall", believing that it might have been the audience hall of the ancient Minoan kings. Its walls are decorated with copies of the fabulous frescoes of agile, leaping bull dancers – the most famous images of Knosos.

Storehouses

The storehouses or "magazines" contain giant earthenware jars called *pithoi*, which the Minoans used to store olive oil, olives, grain and other supplies. Such jars, with a capacity of up to 200 litres, were used by later Greeks over the next four millennia, and are still made today.

South Portico

5 The imposing south gateway to the palace complex has been partially restored, and is decorated with copies of the flowing Procession fresco, the original of which (like the other dazzling finds from Knosos) may be seen in the Irakleio Archaeological Museum *(see pp14–15)*. The roof of this porch was originally supported by four tapering wooden columns.

Plan of Knosos

Great Staircase

6 Three smaller stairways and a maze of corridors would once have led off the five broad, shallow stone steps of the grand staircase. Four of these wide steps survive, and a copy of the original Shield fresco which was found here decorates this part of the palace complex.

Hall of Double Axes

7 The hallway leading to the King's chamber is named after the double-bladed axe symbols *(above)* carved into its walls and columns. The double axe was a characteristic symbol of Knosos and its empire.

North Entrance Passage

8 A fresco of a charging bull, one of the enduring symbols of Knosos, adorns the entrance to this passage. Either side of the entrance are ruined chambers and deep stone storage pits. Images of sacred bulls outlasted the enigmatic Minoan civilization and helped foster the legend of the Minotaur.

Throne Room

9 Here, a stone throne – supposedly that of King Minos – stands next to a basin. The basin is believed to have been used for ritual purification, perhaps before sacrifices were made to honour the gods.

Bust of Sir Arthur Evans

10 A bust of Evans stands at the site entrance, honouring the man who first traced the legendary palace of King Minos to this hillside above Irakleio. His broad reconstructions of the ancient palace owe much to his imagination.

 Many of the exhibits at Knosos are copies – the originals are preserved at the Irakleio Archaeological Museum See pp14–15

Left **Central Court, Knosos** Centre **Horns of Consecration, Knosos** Right **View of Gournia**

Archaeologists in Crete

1 Arthur Evans
Arthur Evans was born into a wealthy British family and educated at Oxford, where he later became keeper of the prestigious Ashmolean Museum. Crete's liberation from Turkish rule in 1897, three years after his first visit to the site, made it possible for him to begin work in 1900, and he devoted the next three decades to Knosos.

2 Harriet Boyd-Hawes
Harriet Boyd (Boyd-Hawes following her marriage) arrived on Crete in 1901 and, after hunting for promising sites, surprised the archaeological world by unearthing at Gournia a complete Minoan town *(see pp30–31)*.

3 Nikolaos Platon
The instincts of Greek archaeologist Nikolaos Platon led to the rediscovery in 1961–2 of the unplundered, overlooked palace site at Zakros *(see p35)*. The important clue was the natural harbour – Platon suspected the site had once been an important trading city.

Agia Triada

4 John Pendlebury
Pendlebury, who continued Evans's work at Knosos, is one of the most colourful figures in Cretan archaeology. He explored much of the island on foot and by donkey, pinpointing dozens of important sites. He also became a hero to Cretans after dying in action against the invading Germans in 1941.

5 Federico Halbherr
An Italian, Halbherr came to Crete in 1884 and befriended the Cretan archaeologist Joseph Hadzidakis, with whom he discovered the Bronze Age relics at the Diktian Cave *(see p80)*. He later unearthed the palace sites at Phaestos *(see pp20–21)* and Agia Triada *(see p81)*.

6 Richard Seager
Among the first American scholars to work in Crete, where at the beginning of the 20th century he excavated the Minoan site at Vasiliki, before starting work at Mochlos *(see p105)*, where American archaeologists are still at work together with Greek researchers.

7 Joseph Hadzidakis
Crete's own Joseph Hadzidakis pioneered the search for relics of the island's distant past, winning permission from the Ottoman sultan to set up the Cretan Archaeological Society in the 1880s. The Society played a key role in locating and preser-

For more on the ancient sites in Crete See pp34–5

Phaestos

ving Crete's important sites, and in setting up the Irakleio Archaeological Museum *(see pp14–15)*.

Alan Wace
8 The prominent director of the British School at Athens, Wace clashed with the opinionated Arthur Evans when his discoveries at Mycenae on the mainland led him to claim (correctly) that the Mycenaean culture had not been an offshoot of the Minoan but had existed independently and eventually had come to control Knosos.

Minos Kalokairinos
9 Cretan businessman and amateur archaeologist Kalokairinos began the first dig at Knosos in 1878, finding fragments of Mycenaean pottery and large pottery storage jars. His discoveries brought Knosos to the attention of Heinrich Schliemann.

Heinrich Schliemann
10 A rich and famous archaeologist fascinated with the world of Homer's epics, he discovered first the site of ancient Troy (in Turkey), then Mycenae (in mainland Greece). In 1887 he turned his attention to Crete, but died before his researches could bear fruit, leaving the field open for Arthur Evans.

The Discovery of Knosos

Bust of Sir Arthur Evans

Arthur Evans was inspired to dig at Knosos by the great German archaeologist Heinrich Schliemann, whose death in 1890 prevented him from excavating the site of what he was convinced was a major Minoan palace. Evans, who excavated the long-lost Minoan palace at Knosos between 1900 and 1929, stands accused by some archaeologists of having used rather too much imagination in his reconstruction of the site, and especially of the upper floor which he dubbed the "Piano Nobile". That said, Evans was attempting to bring to life a site whose origins were lost in the mists of time, and his guesswork is perhaps excusable. Along with the brilliant artistry of the long dead Minoan fresco-painters whose work decorates the walls, his lively imagination at least makes Knosos one of the most colourful and fascinating ruins in Greece.

Queen's Bath
The reconstruction of the clay bath is typical of the conjecture about the function of the rooms at Knosos. Minoan civilization was clearly sophisticated, but did the bath really belong to a queen, as Evans claimed?

Irakleio

A massive medieval fortress still guards the harbour where the galleys of the Serene Republic of Venice once moored. Centuries-old churches and drinking fountains are other reminders of Irakleio's Venetian era. Busy open-air markets and the island's most fascinating museum are also attractions. Find a café table on one of the recently restored central squares and watch the busy everyday life of a small Greek town, or browse the markets for Cretan antiques and delicacies to take home.

Venetian Arsenal
The great wooden war-galleys that gave Venice its maritime supremacy were built and repaired in vaulted arcades *(above)* on the harbourfront opposite the fortress. Wooden fishing boats are still hauled up here for maintenance.

Plateia Venizelou

🕐 To see the market at its best, arrive early, when the stalls are still piled high. The market remains open all day, Monday to Saturday, but most produce traders have packed up by midday.

🍺 Plateia Venizelou is lined with pavement cafés and a good place for a cold drink and a rest after a morning exploring the market and city.

Map K3 • Greek National Tourism Organisation, 1 Xanthoudidou • 28102 46299 • Summer: 8:30am–7:30pm Tue–Sun, noon–7:30pm Mon; Winter: 8:30am–5:30pm Tue–Sun, noon–5:30pm Mon

Top 10 Sights

1. Archaeological Museum
2. Venetian Fortress (Koules)
3. Venetian Arsenal
4. Historical Museum of Crete
5. Morosini Fountain
6. Market
7. Museum of Religious Art
8. Natural History Museum
9. Museum of the Battle of Crete
10. Venetian Bastions

Archaeological Museum
Irakleio's Archaeological Museum is one of the finest in Greece, with finds from ancient Minoan, Greek and Roman cities *(above; see pp13–14)*.

Venetian Fortress (Koules)
The massive walls of the square fortress – the most imposing historic building in Irakleio – were strengthened by the Venetians as the Turkish threat grew during the 16th century.

Irakleio harbour

Historical Museum of Crete
The museum's proudest possession is the only painting by El Greco to have been retained in the artist's native Crete. There are also some lovely stone pieces *(below; see p83)*.

For a morning's walk in Irakleio **See pp82–3**

Morosini Fountain
5 Carved stone lions, the symbol of St Mark, decorate a small fountain *(above)* in the hub of Irakleio's old quarter. It is named after a great 17th-century Doge of Venice. Sadly, it is often dry.

Market
6 The old market has striped awnings and counters piled high with everything from live snails to a myriad varieties of olive *(right)*.

Museum of Religious Art
7 The world's finest collection of Cretan icons is displayed in a pretty 15th-century church *(below)*. Colourful, glowing depictions of saints and martyrs, some of them in elaborate silver frames, adorn the walls. There are three works by Michailis Damaskinos: the *Adoration of the Magi, Last Supper*, and *Christ Appearing to the Holy Women*.

Natural History Museum
8 Offers an impression of the Cretan landscape in Minoan times, before the importation of palm trees, eucalyptus and bougainvillea. There are also stuffed animals, fossils and crystals.

Museum of the Battle of Crete
9 This small collection highlights the German invasion of 1941 and the Cretan resistance to German occupation from 1941–45. There are photographs, documents, weapons and uniforms.

Venetian Bastions
10 Irakleio's Venetian walls *(above)* are surprisingly intact, though among a concrete tide of modern buildings. The best place to appreciate the fortifications is from outside the Chania Gate, with its elaborate carving. Next to it is the massive Pantokratoros Bastion.

Irakleio's Story
The Saracens who occupied Crete in the 9th and 10th centuries built a stronghold on the site of an earlier Roman-Greek settlement named Irakleio after the Greek hero Herakles (Hercules). Under Venetian rule, the name was corrupted into Candia. It reverted to its original name after independence from Turkey. The city was heavily damaged by bombing during World War II, but rose again to become Crete's official capital in 1971.

🔟 Irakleio Archaeological Museum

Founded in 1937 to house the growing treasury of finds from Crete's newly rediscovered archaeological sites, Irakleio's Archaeological Museum gives a dazzling insight into the marvels of the first sophisticated European civilization, which flourished here more than 3,000 years ago. Among the most famous and striking exhibits are the frescoes from Knosos, jewellery, symbol seals and Minoan double axes, as well as the enigmatic Phaestos Disc, with its symbols written by people of the ancient world.

Façade of the Archaeological Museum

🕐 In 2001 work began on an extensive reorganization of the museum. The creation of a new lower floor has revealed remnants of ancient buildings. Some exhibits, including the Giamalakis Collection, may not be on display while the excavations are still being undertaken.

🍴 Plateia Eleftherias, near the museum, is now pedestrianized and has a row of café terraces.

Plateia Eleftherias/1 Xanthoudidou 711, Irakleio • 2810 224630 • Noon–5pm Mon, 8:30am–5pm Tue–Sun • Adm for temporary exhibitions €4; concessions €2

Top 10 Exhibits

1. Hall of Frescoes
2. Ayia Triada Sarcophagus
3. Phaestos Disc
4. Bull's Head Rhyton
5. Faience Figurines of the Snake Goddess
6. Jug of Reeds
7. Minoan Jewellery and Helmets
8. Town Mosaic
9. Gaming Board
10. Miniature Figures

Hall of Frescoes

The most exciting and impressive of the museum's displays are the lively, colourful frescoes from Knosos, Agia Triada and other palaces. They seem to offer a real link between the past and present.

Phaestos Disc

The secret of this clay disc *(above)*, embossed with symbols believed to be the earliest example of a form of printing, has yet to be revealed. The hieroglyphics on the disc, which was found at Phaestos in 1903, are the earliest known Minoan script.

Ayia Triada Sarcophagus

The elaborately painted stone coffin is adorned with depictions of animal sacrifices, a funeral procession *(below)*, women and goddesses riding chariots pulled by slaves and mythical beasts. It was perhaps made for a Minoan ruler.

Share your travel recommendations on **traveldk.com**

4 Bull's Head Rhyton

This 16th-century BC wine vessel *(right)* is carved from black steatite stone and has gilded horns, rock crystal eyes and a mother-of-pearl snout. It was discovered at Knosos and probably used in ritual.

6 Jug of Reeds

With its dark pattern of reeds painted on a lighter back-ground, the graceful pottery jug is the finest example of work from the New Palace era (1700–1450 BC).

5 Faience Figurines of the Snake Goddess

Found at Knosos, the figures *(left)* carry a snake in either hand, as do some later depictions of the goddess Astarte, suggesting some continuity between ancient Crete and later Hellenic cultures.

7 Minoan Jewellery and Helmets

Gold necklaces, rings, ear-rings *(above)*, seals, sword hilts and helmets are among the treasure trove of finds from Knosos, Phaestos and Gortys.

8 Town Mosaic

Glazed tiles, each depicting multi-storey buildings of the Minoan era, were originally part of a mural decoration which may have graced the wall of a palace.

9 Gaming Board

A decorative gaming board, elaborately inlaid and decorated with rock crystal, gold and silver leaf, turquoise paste and ivory, shows that ancient Crete had a wealthy, leisured class as well as trade links with other ancient civilizations.

Museum Guide

The ground-floor galleries (Rooms 1–13) are arranged chronologically, anti-clockwise, beginning with Neolithic finds through to the Roman era. Rooms 14–18, including the Giamalakis Collection, are on the first floor. However, during the current modernization programme, the collections are subject to temporary reorganization and closure.

Key

 Ground floor

First floor

10 Miniature Figures

Doll-like figurines of people and animals look like toys but are believed to have had a religious purpose as votive offerings. Most were found in mountain sanctuaries and caves, such as the Diktian (Psychro) Cave *(see p80)*.

Chania

Chania is Crete's prettiest (and second largest) town, with colourful old Venetian buildings ringing a sheltered harbour that is guarded by sturdy fortifications. To the south are the treeless peaks of the Lefka Ori (White Mountains), sometimes snow-covered to June. Good beaches lie to the west and on the Akrotiri peninsula to the east. As well as Venetian ramparts and churches, a scattering of old Turkish buildings are reminders of the 250 years of Turkish rule.

Municipal Market

Café on Kondylaki

🛍 Chania is the best shopping spot on Crete. Designer beachwear and silver jewellery are in shops on Chalidon and the harbour. Cretan-style leather boots are found in cobbler's shops on Skridlof. The Cretan House Folklore Museum sells beautiful handicrafts.

🍴 The priciest and noisiest restaurants line Akti Koundouriotou, the harbour esplanade. For cheap eats, try the streets east of Plateia Sindrivani.

Map D2 • Chania Tourist Office, Megaro Pantheo, Kriari 40 28210 92943, 8am–2:30pm Mon–Fri • Firkas Nov–Mar: 9am–2pm daily; Apr–Oct: 9am–4pm daily • Museums Tue–Sun • Market 7am–noon Mon–Sat

Top 10 Sights

1. Firkas
2. Chania Archaeological Museum
3. Municipal Market
4. Cretan House Folklore Museum
5. Mosque of the Janissaries
6. Byzantine Collection
7. Etz Hayyim Synagogue
8. Schiavo Bastion and Venetian Walls
9. Lighthouse
10. "Oasis Beach"/Kalamaki

Firkas
Built to guard the harbour, this massive bastion now houses an eclectic Naval Museum *(above)*, including a display about the Battle of Crete.

Chania Archaeological Museum
The excellent collection includes Minoan pottery and clay tablets, Classical and Hellenistic sculpture and glassware, and some fine mosaics *(right)*.

Atmospheric alleyway in Chania

Municipal Market
The market, housed in a 19th-century building, is best visited first thing in the morning. Local farm produce is piled high, including weird-looking fish on beds of ice. There is every imaginable variety of olive, herb and spice.

Previous pages **Rethymno harbour**

4 Cretan House Folklore Museum

With its excellent collection of tools, looms, spinning wheels, rugs, wall hangings and embroidery, this museum reveals and preserves traditional Cretan village skills (see also p39).

5 Mosque of the Janissaries

The Turks built this multi-domed building (above) to set their stamp on Crete after the conquest of 1645. It is the oldest Ottoman building on the island.

6 Byzantine Collection

Next to the Firkas, the Byzantine Collection covers the 1,000-year history of the Byzantine Empire, with displays of coins, jewellery and statuary, mosaics and some fine icons.

7 Etz Hayyim Synagogue

Recently restored, the 15th-century synagogue was used by Chania's Jewish population until the German occupation of 1941–45, when they were deported to death camps by the Germans. A plaque bears the names of 376 Jews who died when a deportees' ship was inadvertently sunk by a British submarine.

9 Lighthouse

Walk out to the little lighthouse at the tip of the Venetian harbour wall (above) for a fine view of the waterfront, harbour entrance and city.

8 Schiavo Bastion and Venetian Walls

The massive Schiavo Bastion and the high walls either side of it are the best preserved of the landward section of the Venetian fortifications, built in the mid-15th century as the threat of Turkish invasion loomed. (No public access.)

10 "Oasis Beach" / Kalamaki

The beach, between the Chrissi Akti headland and Kalamaki, about 3 km (2 miles) from the city centre, is the best near Chania, with its long curve of sand and shingle, cafés and restaurants, parascending and water sports.

Chania's Story

Chania's earliest settlers were Minoans. Later, in 520 BC, colonists from Samos arrived. From 1252 until 1645 it was mainly ruled by the Venetians, who fortified the town and harbour. However, Chania fell in 1645 after a 55-day siege and remained in Turkish hands until 1898. In World War II, Cretan civilians fought alongside Greek and British Commonwealth troops. The German garrison in Chania held out until May 1945.

TOP 10 Phaestos

While Arthur Evans was reconstructing Knosos, the more meticulously scientific Italian scholar Federico Halbherr was unearthing the sites of two Minoan palaces at Phaestos, on a hilltop above the fertile farmlands of the Messara Plane. Most of the ruins visible today are remnants of the later palace (known as the Second Palace), built around 1600 BC and destroyed, possibly by a tidal wave, in around 1450 BC.

Central Court
This vast courtyard *(above)*, formerly flanked on two sides by covered walkways, may have been a parade ground. Niches, perhaps for sentries, are recessed into walls by the main entrance.

Grand Stairway

◯ The on-site Tourist Pavilion at Phaestos serves cold drinks and indifferent food, but there are several better (and cheaper) refreshments stops at Agios Ioannis village, including the Taverna Agios Ioannis, on the main street.

◔ For an overnight stop, head for the little resort of Matala, with sandy beaches and small hotels, less than 30 minutes drive from Phaestos.

• Map H5 • 8km (5 miles) west of Moires village • 28920 42315
• Jun–Oct: 8:30am–7pm daily; Nov–May: 8:30am–3pm daily
• Adm €6.00

Top 10 Sights

1. West Courtyard and Theatre Area
2. Grand Stairway
3. Central Court
4. Peristyle Hall
5. Archive
6. Storerooms and Pithoi
7. First Palace Remains
8. Palace Workshops
9. Classical Temple
10. Royal Apartments

West Courtyard and Theatre Area
Tiers of stone seats *(below)* occupy the north side of the West Court-yard, a paved space that was used for rituals and theatrical ceremonies, including, perhaps, the bull-vaulting depicted in some Minoan frescoes. South of the courtyard are two well-like stone-lined pits used for storing grain, and in the northeast corner are the remains of a shrine which was part of the earlier palace.

Grand Stairway
This broad, monumental stairway leads from the West Courtyard up to the remains of a propylon, or portico, and into a colonnaded lightwell. This was the main entrance to the palace.

Peristyle Hall
The stumps of columns lining this square space indicate that it was once a colonnaded courtyard. Beneath it are traces of an even more archaic building, dating from what is known as the Prepalatial period (3500–1900 BC).

Archive
This row of mud-brick coffers may have been the filing department. The Phaestos Disc, with its undeciphered hieroglyphics, was discovered here. It can be seen in the Irakleio Archaeological Museum *(see pp14–15)*.

Plan of Phaestos

Storerooms and Pithoi
The storerooms *(above)* were where essentials such as grain, oil, wine and olives were kept in huge ceramic jars called *pithoi*. Several *pithoi* remain in the storerooms.

First Palace Remains
To the southeast of the site, the smaller ruins of the First Palace are fenced off for their protection. The palace was built c.1900 BC and destroyed about 200 years later.

Palace Workshops
The remains of a sophisticated kiln or bronze-smith's furnace stand in a large courtyard. Off the courtyard are small chambers which may have been workshops for the palace artisans.

Classical Temple
The remnants of a small temple built during the Classical era provide evidence that Phaestos was still lived in some 1000 years after the mysterious collapse of the Minoan civilization.

Royal Apartments
Now fenced off, these rooms were the grandest in the complex, consisting of the Queen's Chamber, the King's Chamber, a lustral basin (covered pool), and even a bathroom and lavatory with running water *(above)*.

Minoan Demise
What caused the sudden collapse of the Minoan civilisation? Many believe that it was the eruption of the volcano on the island of Thira (Santorini), which would have triggered great tidal waves and suffocating clouds of volcanic ash. Other explanations include invasion by the warlike Mycenaeans of the mainland. But all such theories remain speculative for now.

Rethymno

Rethymno, Crete's third largest town, has been occupied since Minoan times and flourished under Venetian rule. Built on a wide, shallow bay, it has a good beach at the heart of town, and an old quarter crammed with the tall windows and wrought-iron balconies of old-fashioned Venetian and Turkish houses. Several well-preserved mosques are relics of the Turkish era, and, along with the palm trees planted along its seafront esplanade, give the town a pleasantly exotic atmosphere.

Venetian Gate

🕐 Visit Rethymno in July to enjoy the annual wine festival in the public gardens.

🍽 Rethymno's bustling harbour front caters almost exclusively for tourists. Head for the quiet alleys of the old quarter for cheaper, less crowded and often more authentically Cretan restaurants.

Map F3 • Rethymno Tourist Information Office, Sofokli Venizelou 28310 29148 • Apr–Oct: 8:30am–2:30pm Mon–Fri • Fortress 10am–5pm daily (last entry: 4:15pm) • Adm €4; family ticket €10; over 65s €3; children, students and disabled visitors free • Museums Tue–Sun

Top 10 Sights

1. Venetian Fortress
2. Historical and Folk Art Museum
3. Nerandzes Mosque
4. Rethymno Archaeological Museum
5. Rimondi Fountain
6. Venetian Loggia
7. Municipal Gardens
8. Inner Harbour
9. Venetian Gate
10. Beach

1 Venetian Fortress (Fortezza)
Built in 1573, this imposing stronghold – one of the largest Venetian castles ever built – broods on a headland above the town. It has four sturdy bastions and three gates. Within the walls, the most interesting building is the Ibrahim Han Mosque *(below)*, originally the Venetian Cathedral *(see p40).*

2 Historical and Folk Art Museum
Vivid woven rugs and hangings *(above)*, fine lace, traditional pottery and magnificent silver and amber jewellery are among the relics of a vanished way of life preserved in this small museum. Richly decorated textiles from the Franzeskaki collection are also displayed.

Rethymno's inner harbour

3 Nerandzes Mosque (Odeion)
Rising above the old town's rooftops, the pointed minaret of the 17th-century Nerandzes Mosque is a prominent landmark of Rethymno. It is now a music college. Once a Latin church, it was converted into a mosque by the Turks, who replaced the roof with cupolas and the bell tower with a minaret.

For a morning's itinerary in Rethymno See pp94–5

4 Rethymno Archaeological Museum

Opposite the main gate of the fortress, in a converted bastion (part of the fortifications added by the Turks), the archaeological museum's displays include finds from Neolithic, Minoan and Roman sites (left; see p36).

5 Rimondi Fountain

Water flows from an ornate fountain, built in 1626 by one of Rethymno's patrician families on the site of an earlier, simpler water source. Both Venetians and Turks endowed various cities with numerous public fountains.

6 Venetian Loggia (Lotzia)

The most important architectural reminder of Venice's long reign (above) is now a shop selling museum-grade reproductions of Classical works of art.

7 Municipal Gardens

In the summer months the gardens host a popular wine festival and are a good place to begin a walk or to escape the intense heat. The remains of an old Muslim cemetery here were covered by the gardens in 1924.

8 Inner Harbour

The small inner harbour, below the fortress, is one of the most picturesque in Greece, with ramshackle old houses, small boats at anchor and a busy quayside.

9 Venetian Gate (Porta Guora)

The only remnant of the city's Venetian fortifications is an arched stone gate, leading from the picturesque old quarter into the modern part of the city. Other gates were dismantled to provide better vehicle access.

10 Beach

Rethymno's town beach (above) starts just east of the main harbour breakwater and stretches eastward. Behind it is an esplanade lined with palm trees planted in the 1990s, and an almost continuous chain of open-air cafés and restaurants.

Muslims and Hajis

Rethymno's many Turkish features hint at a multi-ethnic past. Until Crete's independence in 1908, the town had a large Turkish Muslim population. Many later moved to Rhodes, which was then still under Turkish rule. The common Cretan name prefix "Hadzi" is a reminder of that era, originally indicating a Cretan who had made the pilgrimage ("Haj" in Turkish/Arabic) to the Holy Land.

Gortys

The ruins of Gortys, in the middle of the fertile Messara plain, date from a much later era than Crete's Minoan palaces. The large site, surrounded by trees, is less crowded than Crete's other top archaeological attractions, though it is just as impressive. It was probably first settled by the Minoans, but flourished later during the period of the Dorian city-states in the 6th century BC. In the 2nd century BC, Gortys defeated its rival Phaestos to become the leading Cretan city.

The Nymphaeum

🌀 To combine your visit to Gortys with an afternoon swim or an overnight stop, drive to Matala, 30 km (20 miles) east of Gortys, which has a fine sandy beach.

🍴 Instead of using the rather spartan on-site cafeteria at Gortys, head for the nearby village of Agioi Deka, where there are several pleasant tavernas and a historic church.

Map J5 • 1 km (half a mile) from Agioi Deka
• 28920 31144
• 8:30am–3pm daily
• Adm €4.00; concessions €2.00

Top 10 Sights

1. Basilica of Agios Titos
2. Roman Odeion and Code of Laws
3. Praetorium
4. Temple of Pythian Apollo
5. Roman Baths
6. Temple of Isis and Serapis
7. Museum
8. Roman Amphitheatre
9. Roman Agora
10. Acropolis (Kastro)

Basilica of Agios Titos

The impressive remains of the tree-aisled basilica *(above)* indicate that Christianity was already well established on the island by the 5th century, when the basilica was built. It is named after St Titus (Agios Titos), who accompanied St Paul the Apostle to Crete in AD 59 and became the first bishop of Crete.

Roman Odeion and Code of Laws

Built into the walls of a Roman odeion are stone slabs inscribed with a code of laws *(above)*, dating from about 500 BC. This is regarded as Gortys' most significant archaeological feature.

Praetorium

A courtyard and stumps of marble columns *(above)* are all that remain of the palace of the Roman governor of Crete and Libya.

Temple of Pythian Apollo

Built in the 7th century BC, the temple had a monumental altar added in the Hellenistic period and was converted into a Christian church in the 2nd century AD.

5 Roman Baths
Remnants of the baths, which would have been a social hub of the Roman city, can be seen among olive groves south of the Praetorium.

6 Temple of Isis and Serapis
Ancient Crete had links with ancient Egypt, as shown by the remains of this temple dedicated to the Egyptian deities.

7 Museum
A collection of marble statuary unearthed at Gortys is on display in a small pavilion on the site, though many of the more impressive finds are held at the Irakleio Archaeological Museum (see pp14 15). The on-site collection includes images of gods, emperors and Roman notables (above).

Plan of the site

8 Roman Amphitheatre
The Roman amphitheatre (above) is surprisingly small for a settlement as important as Roman Gortys, but its tiers of stone seats are well preserved and it is easy to imagine it in use as a venue for drama, oratory or gladiatorial combat.

9 Roman Agora
An impressive statue of the god of healing, Asklepios (now in Irakleio Archaeological Museum), was discovered at the Roman Agora. The agora, or marketplace, was the heart of any ancient Greco-Roman city.

10 Acropolis (Kastro)
Outside the main site, formidable Roman ramparts (below) and a small tower, known as the Kastro ("castle") stand guard on a low hilltop. Come here for a bird's-eye view of Gortys and the countryside.

Byzantine Gortys

After the Roman conquest of 65 BC, Gortys became capital of the Roman province of Crete and Cyrene (modern Libya). It continued to flourish as an important Byzantine provincial hub until, with the weakening of the Byzantine empire, it was sacked by Saracen invaders in the late 7th century AD. It was finally abandoned by its inhabitants in 824.

🔟 Samaria Gorge

The Samaria Gorge, which cuts its way through the Lefka Ori (White Mountains) from the Omalos Plateau to the Libyan Sea, is one of the most striking areas of natural beauty in Greece. Peaks soar on both sides of the gorge, flanked by pine woods and wildflower meadows. Beginning 1,250 m (4,100 ft) above sea level, it emerges on the coast close to the little village of Agia Roumeli after passing through the narrow Sideresportes or "Iron Gates".

Wild goat

🐐 Though fit walkers can complete the 11-mile (17-km) trek in about five hours, it is best to allow eight, including a break of at least an hour. Rest in the hottest part of the day in summer.

🥤 Take plenty of water – at least one litre per person. There are designated rest areas where you can picnic in the shade, and at Agia Roumeli there are small tavernas for your recuperation.

• Map C4 • Gorge open May–mid-Oct (weather permitting – it is advisable to phone first to check) 7am–7pm daily
• Forest Guardhouse, Xyloskalo (28210) 67179
• Forest Guardhouse, Agia Roumeli (28250) 91254 • Admission charge €5.00 • Keep your date-stamped ticket, which you must hand in at the Agia Roumeli gate as you leave

Top 10 Sights

1. Xyloskalo
2. Gigilos and Volakia Peaks
3. Neroutsiko – Riza Sikias
4. Church of Agios Nikolaos
5. Samaria
6. Osia Maria
7. Sideresportes
8. Tarra (Old Agia Roumeli)
9. New Agia Roumeli
10. Agios Pavlos Beach

1 Xyloskalo
The zig-zag path down through the gorge is called the Xyloskalo. The toughest part plummets a breathtaking 1,000 m (3,300 ft) in little more than 2 km (1 mile), passing through pine and cypress woods along the way.

2 Gigilos and Volakia Peaks
Above the Xyloskalo to the west, the skyline is dominated by the massive peaks of Gingilos and Volakia. These mountaintops may remain snow covered well into early summer when the temperatures at sea level are scorching.

3 Neroutsiko and Riza Sikias
The springs of Neroutsiko and Riza Sikias meet at the foot of the Xyloskalo. In winter they form a fierce torrent that makes the gorge impassable, but in summer they dry to a trickle.

4 Church of Agios Nikolaos
Not far from the foot of the Xyloskalo and the springs, the tiny, roughly built chapel of Agios Nikolaos stands in the shade of pine and cypress trees, next to an official rest area.

Plan of the Gorge

Samaria
The last dwellers in the gorge abandoned this village in 1962 when the area was designated a national park. The ghostly cottages have become ever more derelict.

Osia Maria
Dwarfed by steep cliffs, the small church of Osia Maria contains 14th-century frescoes and lends its name to the village of Samaria and to the gorge itself.

Sideresportes
Near the shrine of Afendis Christos, the gorge narrows to just 3 m (9 ft) of space separating rocky walls that rise 700 m (over 2,000 ft).

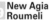

Tarra (Old Agia Roumeli)
A crumbling Turkish fort, a ruined Venetian church and a few tumbledown cottages are all that remain of the old village of Agia Roumeli. Below these ruins lies the site of the small Hellenistic city state of Tarra.

New Agia Roumeli
The inhabitants of Agia Roumeli abandoned their village in the 1960s, intent on a new location by the sea. The new village has since grown into a cheerful string of tavernas and guesthouses spread out along a single street.

Agios Pavlos Beach
Just east of Agia Roumeli, Agios Pavlos beach is a long, uncrowded stretch of pebbles. It is named after the tiny chapel here dedicated to St Paul.

Getting Around
Several tour companies run daily escorted walks, which include transport to and from the gorge. There are also regular buses from Chania to Omalos, 1 km (half a mile) from Xyloskalo. Independent walkers must report to the Forest Guardhouse at Xyloskalo before setting out. There are many guesthouses in Agia Roumeli, and while no roads service this stretch of coast, ferries run daily to Chora Sfakion and Sougia.

The Amari Valley and Mt Idi

The remote Amari Valley, overlooked by the summit of Mt Idi, is one of the most scenic regions in Crete, dotted with tiny village churches – some of them more than 700 years old – and olive groves and vineyards. This upland region is surprisingly fertile, thanks to topsoil washed from the surrounding slopes, and in the Byzantine era was among the wealthiest regions in Crete. A heartland of the Cretan resistance struggle in World War II, many of its villages were destroyed by the Germans in retaliation for attacks by Cretan guerrillas.

Fresco at Agia Anna, near Amari village

Panagia at Thronas

Amari is the best base for exploring the valley and surrounding mountains on foot. There are several tavernas, rooms to rent and a post office where you can change money.

Guided fossil-hunting and herb-gathering walks around the Amari Valley are organized by Lamvros Papoutsakis in Thronos village (28330 22760).

Map G–H4 • Greek National Tourism Organization, Sofokli Venizelou, Rethymno • 28310 29148

Top 10 Sights

1. Mt Idi (Psiloritis) Summit
2. Idaian Cave
3. Amari Village
4. Kamares Cave
5. Hromonastiri
6. The Memorial to Peace
7. Thronos
8. Moni Asomaton
9. Agios Ioannis Theologos
10. Fourfouras

1 Mt Idi (Psiloritis) Summit

Towering above the remote valley, the 2,456-m (8,060-ft) peak of Mt Idi, also called Ida and Psiloritis, is the highest mountain in Crete. Marked walking trails *(see p53)* lead to the summit from the Nida Plateau, 23 km (14 miles) by road from Anogeia village.

2 Idaian Cave

According to Greek myth, Zeus, chief of the Olympian gods, was raised in this enormous cavern *(below)*, 20 minutes' walk from the Nida Plateau. In ancient times this was a place of pilgrimage. Artifacts such as bronze shields, which were left as offerings to Zeus in the 8th century BC, are in the Irakleio Archaeological Museum. The cavern is open daily.

Amari Village

A Venetian clocktower *(right)* on the main square is one of the older buildings in the valley. Just outside the village, some of Crete's oldest Christian frescoes, dated 1225, are in Agia Anna church.

Kamares Cave

This cave, where remarkable Minoan pottery known as Kamares ware was discovered, is a four-hour trek from Kamares village. This sacred site was dedicated to the goddess Eileithyia.

Hromonastiri

The church of Agios Eftihios, outside the village of Hromonastiri, contains faded frescoes, dating from the 11th century, which may be the oldest of their kind in Crete.

The Memorial to Peace

German artist Karen Raeck's work, to the north of the Nida Plateau, is a winged figure outlined in huge natural stone boulders *(above)*.

Thronos

The 14th-century church of the Panagia at Thronos contains striking frescoes and traces of ancient mosaics. Nearby are the ruins of a Hellenistic city, Sivritis.

Moni Asomaton

The monastery of Asomaton *(left)*, built in the Venetian era, is now deserted and spooky. It stands in a fertile oasis of plane trees, palms and eucalyptus.

Getting Around the Valley

Though the Amari Valley feels remote, there are three buses daily from Rethymno to the two largest villages, Thronos and Amari. With a hired car, it is possible to drive up one side of the Amari Valley and down the other. Of the two roads, the eastern route is the most spectacular.

Agios Ioannis Theologos

The church of St John the Divine, built in the 13th century, stands by the road just north of Kardaki village. The fine frescoes were painted in 1347.

Fourfouras

A pretty village set in stunning mountain scenery, Fourfouras is one of the jumping-off spots for the ascent of Mt Idi and some of the less challenging hikes on the Psiloritis massif.

10 Gournia

Unearthed by the American archaeologist Harriet Boyd Hawes between 1901 and 1904, Gournia is the best preserved Minoan town in Crete, though it receives few visitors. Its layout, with narrow stepped streets and tiny houses, is surprisingly similar to that of Cretan villages to this day. It is also one of the oldest sites, inhabited from around 3000 BC, though the surviving buildings date from the later Second Palace Period. Like other Minoan settlements, it was destroyed by earthquake and fire around 1450 BC. The honeycomb of ruins stands only waist high.

Stairway

Remains of workshops

🌀 Unfortunately, the beaches near Gournia (like most along this stretch of coast) are dirty and unappealing.

🍴 There is nowhere to eat at Gournia. Pachia Ammos, 3 km (2 miles) east, has a string of restaurants on its waterfront.

Map N5 • South of coast road, 18 km (11 miles) east of Agios Nikolaos • 28420 93028 • 8:30am–3pm Tue–Sun • Adm €2.00

Top 10 Sights

1. Courtyard
2. Stairway
3. Central Palace Court
4. Palace
5. Storerooms
6. Shrine
7. Carpenter's Workshop
8. Potter's Workshop
9. Bronzesmith's Workshop
10. Wash Basins

Courtyard
At the southern end of the site an expansive courtyard *(below)* would have been the hub of the settlement and may have been the town's market. It was probably also used for ceremonial purposes.

Stairway
The L-shaped stair that rises from the courtyard to the central court of the palace is characteristic of Minoan palaces. The design of it echoes similar ceremonial stairs found in virtually every Minoan palace site in Crete.

Central Palace Court
Access to the central court of the palace from the courtyard below is by the ceremonial staircase. The Minoan ruler of Gournia may well have used this antechamber to the small palace building *(below)* as his audience hall.

Palace

4 The palace, which may have been the dwelling place of a governor who ruled Gournia on behalf of the Minoan ruler of Knosos, is a miniature version of the more important Minoan royal palaces. In the centre of the palace is a sacrificial altar.

Plan of the site

Storerooms

5 Adjoining the palace are storerooms *(left)*, or magazines, where grain, oil and other essentials would have been kept in earthenware jars.

Shrine

6 A cobbled, mosaic-decorated path leads steeply up to a small shrine, which was found to contain cult objects. The terracotta goddess figurines and snake are now displayed in the Irakleio Archaeological Museum *(see pp14–15)*.

Carpenter's Workshop

7 Gournia was clearly a thriving, self-contained community, and tools and other materials found in this small building indicate that it was used by a woodworker who may also have lived on the premises with his family.

Potter's Workshop

8 Clay fragments indicate this was a potter's workshop *(right)*. The finds unearthed in this and other buildings indicate Gournia was suddenly abandoned rather than slowly run down.

Bronzesmith's Workshop

9 Bronze nails and scraps, and a simple stone anvil suggest a smithy used in smelting bronze. Tools, weapons, utensils and votive objects from Gournia are at Irakleio Archaeological Museum.

Wash Basins

10 The crude stone washing basins found outside almost every building in Gournia are known as *gournes* in modern Greek. They gave their name to the long lost site when it was rediscovered.

Lost Names

Although some Minoan scripts have been deciphered, archaeologists still have no way of knowing what the Minoans called most of their cities. The names by which they are known today stem from words used by the much later Greek settlers who occupied the island long after the collapse of Minoan civilization.

Crete's Top 10

Left **Turkish and Egyptian forces in 1896** Right **Venetian fortress**

Moments in History

1 1750 BC: Golden Age of Minoan Culture

Crete is the centre of the Minoan civilization, which is marked by the building of Knosos and other palaces. Mycenaeans take over Knosos in 1450 BC.

2 Roman Conquest

The first Roman invasion of Crete in 71 BC is repulsed by the Dorian Greeks, but a second attack in 69 BC succeeds. Some Cretan cities side with the invaders, and by 67 BC Crete is firmly in Roman hands.

Cretan statue of Hadrian

3 Byzantine Reconquest

The Byzantine Empire loses Crete to Arab invaders in AD 824. The Emperor Nikiforas Fokas reconquers the island in 961.

4 Venetian Rule

Crete falls into Venetian hands after 1204, when the Fourth Crusade goes awry and the Byzantine Emperor is deposed by an army of Frankish crusaders in alliance with Venice. Cretans rebel against the Venetians, but without success.

5 The Turks

Chania and Rethymno quickly fall to an attack by Turks in 1645. Venetian sea-power enables the Venetian capital of Candia (modern Irakleio) to resist a 21-year siege, but Venice finally surrenders in 1669. The Cretans rise too against the Turks. The first major rebellion begins in 1770 in mountainous Sfakia and is led by Ioannis Daskalogiannis. It ends badly, however, with Sfakia conquered.

6 War of Independence

In 1821 a nationwide rising in mainland Greece flares into a full-scale and eventually successful War of Independence. In Crete, Chatzimichalis Dalianis

Painting by Jan Peeters, said to be of the Siege of Candia in the 17th century

German troops in 1941

and fewer than 400 rebels raise the Greek banner at Frango-kastello, where they are besieged and slaughtered. Crete remains under the Turkish yoke.

1866: Another Rebellion Against Turks
Undaunted by these heroic failures, Crete rises again in 1866, with a self-appointed Cretan Assembly declaring independence and union with Greece. The Turks bring in Egyptian troops to quell the rebels, but in Europe there is growing sympathy for the Cretan cause.

Great Powers Intervene
Several risings in the last decades of the 19th century culminate in the landing of Greek troops in 1897 and international intervention.

Union with Greece
In 1905 Eleftherios Venizelos – a minister in Prince George's governorship of Crete – calls for a nationalist revolution and in 1908 the Cretan Assembly declares union *(enosis)* with Greece.

Occupation and Liberation in World War II
German forces drive the Allies out of Crete in May 1941, but Cretan guerrillas continue to resist. Most German troops flee Greece in autumn 1944 as Allied troops land, but the garrison at Chania holds out until the end of the war in May 1945.

Top 10 Empires and Governments

1 Minoan Empires
The Minoan civilization emerged between 3000 and 1900 BC. A volcanic explosion may have destroyed the Minoan cities around 1450 BC.

2 Mycenaeans
Mycenaean Greeks from the mainland settled in Crete after 1450 BC.

3 The Dorians
Dorian Greeks from northern Greece arrived in the 12th century BC, driving the descendants of the Minoans into remote areas.

4 Dorian City States
Gortys and Kidonia (modern Chania) were among the most powerful.

5 Roman Empire
Gortys (which had sided with Rome) became capital of the province of Crete and Cyrene (modern Libya).

6 Byzantine Empire
In the 4th century AD Crete became part of the Byzantine realm.

7 Arab Conquest
In AD 824–961 Arab forces led by Byzantine general Nicephoros Phokas *(see p56)* overturned Crete.

8 Venetian Empire
In 1204 the Republic of Venice took control of Crete and the Aegean islands.

9 Ottoman Empire
The Ottoman Turks invaded Crete in strength in 1645 and held the island until the end of the 19th century.

10 Kingdom of the Hellenes
Crete was united with Greece in 1913. In 1923, 30,000 Muslim Cretans were expelled from Crete.

Crete's Top 10

Left **Bull fresco, Knosos** Right **Gortys**

🔟 Ancient Sites

1 Knosos
Just outside Irakleio, Knosos is by far the most striking of the ancient Minoan palace ruins on Crete. Dating back more than 3,500 years, it was destroyed, probably by a volcanic eruption, around 1450 BC and not redis-covered until the late 19th century (*see pp8–11*).

2 Phaestos
The ruins of the Minoan palace at Phaes-tos, on a hilltop by the south coast of Crete, are second only to those at Knosos. A maze of walls and courtyards marks the site of the Second Palace at Phaestos, built around 1600 BC. Hieroglyphics on the clay Phaestos Disc still puzzle scientists (*see pp20–21*).

3 Gortys
The ruined city of Gortys, with basilica and remnants of a Roman provincial governor's palace, dates from the early Christian era. The site extends over a wide area, and is usually uncrowded, so it can be explored at leisure (*see pp24–5*).

4 Gournia
The well-preserved Minoan town of Gournia, a maze of roofless stone walls, makes an interesting contrast with the better-known Minoan palac-es. This was a working community, and archaeol-ogists discovered work-shops used by potters, smiths and carpenters alongside tiny houses surrounding a small palace (*see pp30–31*).

Giant pot, Malia

5 Agia Triada
A treasury of Minoan relics, including tablets in-scribed with the still undeci-phered Minoan Linear A script, has been discovered on this site of an L-shaped Minoan villa, built about 1700 BC. The site was later occupied by Mycenaean settlers, who built a *megaron* (chief's hall) and a village with a unique row of porticoed shops. ◈ *3 km (2 miles) west of Phaestos • Map H5 • 28920 91360 • 8:30am–3pm daily • Adm*

6 Malia
East of the busy summer holiday resort of Malia is an archaeol-ogical site of the same

Phaestos

Left **Agia Triada** Right **Malia Archaeological Site**

name. The Minoan double-axe symbol, or *labrys*, is carved into two pillars of a small shrine. Excavations are still going on near the palace site. ☽ *3 km (2 miles) east of Malia • Map M4 • 28970 31597 • 8:30am–3pm Tue–Sun • Adm*

Zakros

The fourth largest of Crete's Minoan palaces, Zakros was rediscovered in 1961 by Cretan archaeologist Nikolaos Platon. The site had not been plundered, and finds included a stunning rock crystal jug, now in the Irakleio Archaeological Museum *(see pp14–15)*. Remains of the palace and a cistern can be seen. ☽ *Kato Zakros • Map R5 • 28430 93338 • 8:30am–3pm Tue–Sun • Adm*

Praisos

This scenic site – with only the remnants of a temple, house foundations and a city wall to be seen – was the last enclave of the Eteocretan ("true Cretan") descendants of the Minoans. It survived until the 2nd century BC,

when it was sacked by Dorians. ☽ *By Nea Praisos village • Map Q5 • Unenclosed • Free*

Itanos

The remains of a Hellenistic wall, foundations of two early Christian basilicas, and toppled walls and columns are the only indications that this was once an important city. It flourished until early medieval times, when it was destroyed by Saracen raiders. ☽ *2 km (1 mile) north of Vai • Map R4 • Unenclosed • Free*

Levin

Ancient Levin, on a hilltop just outside the modern village of Lendas, is now no more than a scattering of ruined walls and pillars around a stone arch. The site was a sanctuary dedicated to Asklepios, the god of healing. From the 3rd century BC to the Christian era it was an important place of pilgrimage. ☽ *North of Lendas • Map J6 • Unenclosed • Free*

Zakros Palace

Left **Chania Museum** Centre **Siteia Museum** Right **Agios Nikolaos Museaum**

Art and Archaeological Museums

1 Irakleio Archaeological Museum

The largest museum in Crete, and well worth visiting. Its collection is currently being reorganized, modernized and expanded *(see pp14–15)*.

Statue from Rethymno Archaeological Museum

2 Chania Archaeological Museum

Housed in a historic building which was first a Venetian church then a Turkish mosque, the museum is packed with Minoan finds, Hellenistic and Roman marble sculpture, pottery and jewellery found at archaeological sites in western Crete. ⚲ *Map D2* • *28210 90334* • *8:30am–3pm Tue–Sun* • *Disabled access* • *Adm*

3 Siteia Archaeological Museum

The most important exhibits are from the palace site at Zakros, on Crete's east coast, which was uncovered in 1961. They include clay tablets inscribed with the symbols of the Minoan Linear A

Gardens, Irakleio Archaeological Museum

script, as well as bronze tools and kitchen utensils. ⚲ *Map Q4* • *Fiskokefalou 3* • *28430 23917* • *8:30am–3pm Tue–Sun* • *Adm*

4 Rethymno Archaeological Museum

In a converted bastion built by the Turks, the collection extends from the Stone Age to the Minoan and Hellenistic eras, with finds from archaeological sites, caves and cemeteries in the Rethymno region. Among the highlights are late Minoan burial caskets, or *larnakes*, and burial goods found in Minoan cemetery sites. ⚲ *Map F3* • *Cheimarras, Fortetza* • *28310 54668* • *8:30am–3pm Tue–Sun* • *Adm*

5 Byzantine Collection of Chania

The fine collection of beautiful Cretan icons is the best reason to visit this small museum next to Chania's harbour fortress. The collection spans 1,000 years of Byzantine history and sheds light on an often ignored chapter in Crete's complex history. ⚲ *Map D2* • *82 Theotokopoulou* • *28210 96046* • *8:30am–3pm Tue–Sun* • *Adm*

6 Agios Nikolaos Archaeological Museum

A jug in the stylized shape of a female figure, found at the Bronze Age site at Korifi and known as the Goddess of Mirtos, is this museum's proudest exhibit.

Elsewhere are clay Minoan coffins decorated with paintings, good examples of Vasiliki pottery and some finely worked gold jewellery.

Skull from Agios Nikolaos Archaeological Museum

❂ Map N4 • K. Palaeologou 74 • 28410 24943 • 8:30am–3pm Tue–Sun • Adm

7 Museum of Religious Art, Irakleio

This 15th-century Venetian church – where both El Greco and the great icon painter Michailis Damaskinos are said to have learned their skills – contains the world's best array of Cretan icons. The collection includes three superb works by Damaskinos. ❂ Map K3 • Church of Agia Ekaterini, Plateia Ag. Ekaterini • 2810 288825 • 9am–1:30pm Mon–Sat, 5–7pm Tue, Thu, Fri • Adm

8 Ierapetra Archaeological Museum

Exhibits include huge clay storage jars (pithoi), Minoan sarcophagi made of clay (larnakes) statues, and bronze weapons and tools dating from the time of the Dorian city-states, when Ierapetra became one of the most powerful cities in eastern Crete. ❂ Map N6 • 1 Kostoula Adrianou Ierapetra • 28420 28721 • 8:30am–3pm Tue–Sun • Adm

9 Archanes Collection

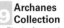

Finds from the Minoan cemetery discovered at Fourni, just north of Archanes village, are displayed in the village's small but rather good archaeological museum along with relics from other nearby sites. ❂ Map K4 • Kalochristianaki, Archanes • 2810 752712 • Summer: 8:30am–2:30pm daily • Adm

10 El Greco Museum

Copies of paintings and biographical material relating to the life of the Cretan-born artist Domenikos Theotokopoulos, better known as El Greco, are displayed in a restored Venetian building in Fodele village, which is claimed to be his birthplace. ❂ Map J3 • Fodele village, just south of main coast road • 2810 521500 • Summer: 9am–7pm Tue–Sun • Adm

Archanes Archaeological Museum

Left **Cretan weaving** Centre **Cretan House Folklore Museum** Right **Gavalochori Historical Museum**

🔟 Folklore Museums

1 Lychnostatis Open Air Museum of Folk Culture

Traditional Cretan ways of life that lasted for centuries only began to die out in recent decades. This lively open-air museum gives some insight into life on the island before tourism, television and the mobile phone. Fascinating exhibits include a windmill and an old stone cottage. ○ Chersonisos • Map L4 • 28970 23660 • 9am–2pm Sun–Fri • Adm (students free)

Lychnostatis Open Air Museum

2 Historical and Folk Art Museum, Rethymno

A small museum housed in a Venetian mansion displays relics of a vanished way of life, including colourful woven artifacts, lace, silver jewellery and ceramics. ○ Vernardou 30 • Map F3 • 28310 23398 • 9:30am–2pm Mon–Sat • Adm

3 Museum of History, Paleochora

This small museum in the centre

Historical and Folk Art Museum, Rethymno

of Paleochora provides a fascinating way to spend an hour or two. It takes as its theme the history of Crete and its people, with exhibits which focus on how living on Europe's border with Africa has influenced events in the past. ○ Centre of village • Map B4 • 28230 42265 • 9am–1pm & 6:30–8:30pm daily • Adm

4 Museum of Cretan Ethnology, Vori

Excellent collection which gives real insight into the hard life of Cretan villagers in years gone by. For example, there are displays on how wild foods – from dandelions to snails – featured in their diet! ○ Vori • Map H5 • 28920 91110 • Apr–Oct: 10am–6pm daily; Nov–Mar: 8:30am–3pm daily • Adm

5 Museum of Rural Life, Piskopiana

Wooden farming tools, an old olive press and a copper raki still are among the exhibits. ○ Outskirts of Limin Chersonisos • Map L3 • 28970 23303 • 10am–7pm daily • Adm

6 Agios Nikolaos Folklore Museum

Overlooking Agios Nikolaos's lagoon-like inner harbour, the museum houses colourful textiles and costumes, plus farming and fishing equipment. ○ Kondilaki 2 • Map N4 • 28410 25093 • 9:30am–1:30pm & 5–9pm Sun–Fri • Adm

Folklore Museum, Anogeia *(see p99)*

7 Arolithos Museum of Agricultural History and Popular Art

This museum is linked with a holiday village which tries to give its guests a taste of traditional Cretan life, with craft workers who use traditional methods, a restaurant and bakery with wood-burning ovens, and live music and dancing in the evening. ⊛ *Arolithos village, 8 km west of Irakleio on old highway • Map J4 • 9am–5pm (to 8pm Apr–Sep) Mon–Fri, 10am–6pm Sat & Sun • Adm*

8 Cretan House Folklore Museum

Traditional looms and spinning wheels, richly coloured rugs, wall hangings and embroidery can be found at this delightful place. ⊛ *46B Chalidon • Map D2 • 28210 91110 • 9am–3pm 6–9pm Mon–Sat • Adm*

9 Folklore and Martial Museum, Somatas

A quirky, two-room museum with a collection of farm tools, early radios and household items in one room, and weapons, medals, uniforms and memorabilia from World War II in the other. Opening hours can be erratic. ⊛ *Somatas, Rethymno • Map F3 • 28310 41315 • 9am–6pm daily • Free but donation welcomed*

10 Historical and Folklore Museum of Gavalochori

This excellent small museum is housed in an old Venetian-Turkish mansion and depicts the history and culture of the village. Highlights include local skills such as silk spinning, masonry and carpentry. ⊛ *Gavalochori village • Map E3 • 28250 23222 • 9am–7pm Mon–Sat, 10am–1:30pm, 5–7pm Sun • Adm*

Traditional Crafts

1 Weaving
Traditional hand looms are still in use, made by skilled craftsmen from cypress, walnut or mulberry wood.

2 Embroidery
Rethymno was a major centre for embroidery, a skill introduced to Crete in the Byzantine era.

3 Spinning
Older village women still spin wool into yarn using a spindle and distaff – a skill that hasn't changed since the time of the Minoans.

4 Musical Instruments
Crete has a strong tradition of making musical instruments *(see pp60–61)* and many places still make the *lyra*, a three-stringed violin, and the *laouta* (mandolin).

5 Church Embroidery
Crete's Orthodox monks and nuns embellish sumptuous church vestments with gold, silver and silk stitching.

6 Wood Carving
Olive, cypress and mulberry yield a hard wood loved by skilled Cretan carpenters.

7 Leatherwork
Everything from shepherds' boots and mule harnesses to satchels, handbags and sheepskin garments.

8 Silversmithing
Silver jewellery and religious objects such as icon frames and crucifixes.

9 Lace
Silk *kopaneli* lace is made by bobbin weaving, a skill revived in Gavalochori.

10 Antique Weapons
The Cretan *pallikar* (warrior-hero) loved highly decorated weapons. Authentic antique weapons are highly valued.

Left **Rethymno** Centre **Spinalonga** Right **Aptera**

Venetian and Turkish Castles

Rethymno
The massive fortress that dominates Rethymno's harbour was built by the Venetians with sloping walls to better deflect the Ottoman Empire's gigantic cannon. But it proved no match for the military ingenuity of the Turks, and fell after a short siege. Ironically, it became a far more successful stronghold for the Turkish Ottomans *(see also p22)*.

Frangokastello bust

Frangokastello
The Venetians built this romantic coastal fortress to defend the south coast from Saracen pirates. In 1821 it was occupied by a small force of Cretan rebels, holding out against a vastly greater Turkish army. The rebels were defeated of course, but, according to legend, once a year their ghosts appear from the sea to reclaim the ruined castle *(see pp59 & 92)*. ◈ Map E4

Spinalonga
A formidable island fortress built in 1579 to command the entrance to the Gulf of Mirabello. Venice managed to hang on to it even after the surrender of Candia (Irakleio) in 1669, and gave it up only by treaty in 1715. After Turkish withdrawal, it was used for a time as a leper colony *(see pp104–105)*.

Chania
The Venetians lost Chania to their arch-rivals, the Genoese, in 1263. They regained it 22 years later, and set about making the town impregnable, starting with walls around the hill above the harbour in the district still known as Kastelli (the castle). Further walls followed, but though they may have deterred occasional pirate raids, they proved ineffective when the Turks assailed the city in 1645. ◈ Map D2

Frangokastello

5 Paleochora

Kastel Selinou, as Paleochora was first known, was built in 1279 to guard the southwest against pirates. The great Turkish corsair Barbarossa destroyed it in 1539. The Turks saw no need to rebuild it, and it has remained an elegant ruin ever since. ✎ Map B4

Siteia's Venetian Fortress

6 Venetian Acropolis and Polyrinia

On a hilltop above Paleokastro, a Venetian keep shares the peak with the ruins of the Hellenistic city of Polyrinia, which thrived until the Saracen invasion of the 9th century. Stone from Hellenistic buildings, already 1,000 years old when the Venetians arrived, seems to have been incorporated into the castle walls. ✎ Map B2

7 Aptera

Climb the bastions of the Aptera Fort, on a hilltop near the ruins of Byzantine Aptera for sweeping views. Below, across the coastal highway, is the grim Itzedin Fort, now a prison and closed to visitors. ✎ Map D2

8 Da Molini Castle Ruins, Alikianos

Though much overgrown, the dilapidated walls standing among orange and lemon trees are still impressive. The castle was the scene of a famous massacre, when the Cretan rebel leader

Georgios Kandanoleon was betrayed by Francesco Molini during his wedding to Molini's daughter. ✎ Map C2

9 Venetian Fortress, Siteia

Siteia's restored Venetian fort is used as an open-air theatre for concerts and plays in summer. The fortress is all that remains of the city's once substantial ring of battlements which resisted a three-year siege by the Turks in 1648–51. ✎ Map Q4

10 Venetian Tower, Finikas, Loutro

The lonely tower standing on a headland between Loutro and the bay of Finix, is yet another Venetian relic. Nearby are a few scattered blocks, the remains of a Byzantine church and also a Hellenistic town, the latter an important seaport when the Romans ruled Crete. ✎ Map D4

Left **Panagia Kera** Centre **Moni Arkadiou** Right **Moni Agia Triada**

Churches and Monasteries

Moni Arkadiou
Though founded in the 5th century, most of the monastic buildings here date from the 16th century. Moni Arkadiou has a special significance for Cretans. During the great revolt of 1866, the monastery - crowded with refugees as well as Cretan freedom fighters - was besieged by the Turks. Rather than surrender, the rebel defenders blew up their gunpowder stores, killing themselves and many of their enemies. Map G4 • 28310 83076 • 8am–1pm, 3:30–8pm daily • Adm

Panagia Kera
The most important Byzantine-era church in Crete, Panagia Kera, was built in the 13th and 14th centuries. The church is dedicated to the Virgin and to saints Anthony and Anna, and is adorned with expressive murals depicting the two saints, as well as 14 scenes portraying the secret life of the Virgin Mary after Christ's Crucifixion and Resurrection. Map N5 • 28410 51525 • 8:30am–3pm daily • Adm

Moni Toplou
The Toplou monastery's forbidding exterior is deceptive, for like many Greek monasteries it was fortified against bandits during the Middle Ages. Inside, however, is a different world of serene, flower-filled courtyards

Moni Toplou

and cloisters, and a church that houses one of the greatest Cretan works of religious art, the icon *Lord, Thou Art Great* by Ioannis Kornaros. Map Q4 • 28430 61226 • 9am–1pm and 2–6pm daily • Adm

Moni Agia Triada
The Monastery of the Holy Trinity stands among its own olive groves, and although its monastic community has dwindled to just a few members, its lovely old buildings are gradually being restored. Visitors are welcome, and the monks will happily sell you some of their home-grown olive oil, which is of high quality. Map D2 • 28210 63310 • 8am–2pm, 5–7pm daily • Adm

Moni Gouverneto
Only three elderly monks remain in this isolated monastery, deep in the wilds of the bleak and barren Akrotiri Peninsula. The building encloses a tranquil courtyard, in which stands a small chapel with some of the oldest frescoes in Crete. Map D2 • 28210 63319 • 9am–noon, 5–7pm Mon, Tue, Thu; 5–11am, 5–8pm Sat & Sun • Adm

Moni Preveli
Built during the 17th century to replace a more remote monastery building, Moni Preveli's peaceful dormitories and cloisters look

Moni Preveli

inward, onto an 18th-century courtyard with a 19th-century church and a small museum. Exhibits include lavishly ornamented vestments, church silver and icons. ◈ *Map F5 • 28320 31246 • 9am–1:30pm, 3:30–7pm • Adm*

Agioi Deka Church

This 13th-century Byzantine Church of the Ten Saints stands on the spot where ten Cretan Christians were martyred by the troops of the Roman Emperor Decius in AD 250. A striking icon depicting the ten saints with golden haloes is displayed in the nave. ◈ *Map J5 • 8am–5pm • Adm*

Moni Chrissopygis

The Convent of the Source of Life, like so many Cretan monasteries, looks more like a castle than a religious dwelling. It is relatively new, built in 1863, and has a studio in which icons are painted using age-old techniques. ◈ *Map C2 • 28210 91125 • 8am–noon and 3:30–6pm daily • Adm*

Moni Katholikou

In a rugged valley riddled with caves once used by hermits, the abandoned monastery of Gouverneto is a ghostly place, with crumbling buildings that seem to have grown out of the rockface. ◈ *Map D2 • Open access*

Agios Nikolaos

This church has a history that reflects Chania's past. It was built by the Venetians, converted into a mosque after the Turkish conquest, and in the early 20th century converted again into a Greek Orthodox church dedicated to St Nicholas. Its minaret is a relic from the centuries of Muslim worship here. ◈ *Map D2 • 8am–7pm daily • Free*

Moni Chrissopygis

Left **Plakias** Centre **Paleochora** Right **Agia Galini**

🔟 Beach Resorts

Georgioupoli

At the mouth of a river, 20 km (13 miles) west of Rethymno, lies Georgioupoli. It's a quiet resort, the hub of the village provided by a taverna- and café-lined square shaded by plane trees. Georgioupoli's hotel and self-catering accommodation is spread out along an expansive sandy beach. ✎ *Map E3*

Cave shrine, Malia

Malia

With its great sandy beach and close proximity to Irakleio International Airport, Malia was destined to become one of the island's liveliest package holiday resorts. In July and August it is thronged, attracting a young crowd with its water sports and after-dark scene. But there are peaceful spots, too. ✎ *Map M4*

Limin Chersonisos

Biggest and busiest of the island's resorts, Limin Chersonisos straddles the north coast highway, a long

double strip of hotels, apartment complexes, bars, restaurants, dance clubs and shops. Catering mainly to package holidaymakers, it has now almost merged with the neighbouring resorts of Stalida and Malia. ✎ *Map L3*

Plakias

A huge sweep of clean grey sand draws visitors to this little south-coast resort, but there are even better beaches nearby at Damnoni, which can be reached by boat or on foot. Plakias is one of the island's quieter beach resorts, and its accommodation mostly takes the form of self-catering apartments. ✎ *Map F4*

Matala

Matala's coves of fine golden sand, surrounded by rocky red cliffs harbouring Roman cave-tombs, made the place a magnet for hippy travellers in the 1960s. Its tourism is more orthodox now, but Matala is still pleasantly low-key. A good base for exploring Gortys and Phaestos. ✎ *Map G6*

Limin Chersonisos

Matala

9 Bali
A small resort, purpose built around coves on the north coast, Bali comes to life in high season, when its "Paradise Beach" glistens with sunbathing bodies. ⊗ *Map H3*

6 Agia Galini
This picturesque south-coast fishing village took to tourism in the 1980s. Its pebbly beach (crowded in high season) is on a crescent bay, where a small river flows through a thicket of reeds into the sea. Places to eat and drink abound. ⊗ *Map G5*

7 Makrigialos
Makrigialos has the best and longest beach in eastern Crete, a swathe of grey sand and shingle beneath pine-covered slopes. The village and its neighbour Analipsi have melded into a single chain of tavernas and guesthouses. ⊗ *Map P5*

8 Paleochora
On a headland crowned by a dilapidated Venetian castle, Paleochora is part fishing village, part resort. It has a crescent of yellow sand on the west side of the promontory and a longer, less crowded pebbly beach on the east. ⊗ *Map B4*

10 Siteia
The beach at Siteia stretches for miles east of the town and is backed by a ramshackle strip of hotels, guesthouses and cafés. This quiet port on Crete's north coast seems to have escaped the tourist invasion relatively unscathed. ⊗ *Map Q4*

Siteia

Left **A beachside taverna at Agia Roumeli** Right **Irakleio harbour**

Top10 Islands and Boat Trips

The island fortress of Spinalonga

Elafonisi
With its sandy beach and vivid blue lagoon, the tiny, tropical-looking island of Elafonisi is barely separable from the Crete shoreline. Daily boat trips from Palaiochora (May–Sep) take an hour each way *(see also p50)*. Map A4

Spinalonga
At the mouth of the Gulf of Mirabello, Spinalonga is a maze of Venetian battlements. Daily boat trips venture here in summer from Plaka, Elounda and Agios Nikolaos – 5, 20 and 35 minutes respectively *(see p104)*.

Gavdos
Europe's southernmost point, where a few simple guesthouses, tavernas and beaches welcome visitors. Boats sail daily in summer from Palaiochora and Chora Sfakion; journey time around 4 hours. Map D6

Palaiochora-Agia Roumeli
The boat from Palaiochora hugs the rugged south coast, calling in at the lazy port of Sougia, before chugging along to Agia Roumeli, a cheerfully ramshackle village at the foot of the Samaria Gorge. Map B–C4

Agia Roumeli-Chora Sfakion
After marching up and down the Samaria Gorge, your journey can be extended along the coast by hopping on one of several daily boats that potter eastwards. All end up at the small port of Chora Sfakion. Map C–E4

The short stretch of water separating Elafonisi from the Crete shoreline

Threshing corn on Gavdos

Koufonisi
Coves and sandy beaches attract boats from Makrygialos, while the remains of a Roman amphitheatre attest to a time when the island grew rich from the trade of murex, a sea mollusc from which imperial purple dye was made. ◈ Map Q6

Chrysi
Chrysi ("Golden"), so named for its sandy beaches, is known locally as Gaidouronisi ("Donkey Island") because of the Cretan habit of retiring elderly donkeys to uninhabited islands. Daily boat trips from Ierapetra take 30–45 minutes in summer. ◈ Map N6

Dia
A group of endangered Cretan wild goats have made their home on Dia. They can be visited on a day trip from Irakleio or Chersonisos. ◈ Map K3

Imeri Gramvousa
This island crag just off the Gramvousa peninsula is crowned by a dramatic, crumbling castle. There are several boat trips each week from Kastelli, and excursions through tour agencies in Chania and Rethymno. ◈ Map B1

Andikithira
If seeking solitude, this remote island could be an ideal stop-off between Crete and mainland Greece to the northwest. A weekly ferry sails between Kastelli, Andikithira, its larger neighbour Kithira and Gythio on the mainland.

Watersports

Windsurfing
Boards are readily available for hire, and the best beaches are Georgioupoli, Chersonisos, Malia, Ierapetra and Plakias.

Snorkelling
Crete's crystal waters, teaming with colourful fish, are ideal for snorkelling.

Banana Rides
Inflatable bananas, towed at high speed and carrying up to half a dozen riders, are big in Malia and Chersonisos.

Sea Biscuit Rides
Similarly popular is the "sea biscuit", a tough inflatable ring for a single rider.

Catamaran Sailing
Catamarans can be hired by the hour or day at most resorts, with instruction available for novice sailors.

Yacht Sailing
Yachts can be chartered "bareboat" (without skipper or crew), fully crewed or with a skipper only. The National Tourism Organisation has a list of charter companies.

Scuba Diving
Although archaeological sites and ancient shipwrecks are off-limits, there are good dives to several wrecks from World War II.

Waterskiing
Waterskiing, though expensive, is available at most of the bigger resorts.

Aquapark
At Chersonisos, the Aqua Splash Water Park is a playground of waterslides, waves and waterfalls.

Jet Skiing
Despite the introduction of rules limiting their use, jet skis can still be rented at all major resorts.

Crete's Top 10

Left **Argyroupoli** Centre **Elos** Right **Hamezi**

10 Villages

1 Kritsa

Sweeping mountain views and a reputation as one of the craft centres of eastern Crete ensures that Kritsa sees its fair share of tourism. Its main street, lined with old stone buildings, is packed with shops selling leather satchels and sandals, embroidery and brightly patterned rugs. Some 30 minutes' walk from Kritsa is the minor archaeological site of Lato, where you can see the remains of a Classical Greek city. *Map M5 • Lato 8:30am–2pm Tue–Sun*

2 Argyroupoli

Western Crete's prettiest mountain village is tucked in the foothills of the Lefka Ori, on the site of the Hellenistic town of Lappa. The slopes of its valley setting flourish with lush greenery, watered by natural springs. Argyroupoli makes a good base for relatively easy walking in the surrounding hills. *Map E4*

3 Axos

About 10 km (6 miles) inland from the main north coast highway on the way to the scenic Amari Valley, Axos has striking views and an attractive Byzantine church dedicated to Agia Anna. The village is a popular stop for excursion groups, and its tavernas and souvenir shops get crowded around lunch time. On the hillside above Axos are a few scattered remnants of an ancient settlement. *Map H4*

4 Kournas

Kournas nestles at the foot of Mt Dafnomadara, in a fertile plain close to Crete's only freshwater lake. Its old stone houses cluster around a steep main street, and the village has two historic Byzantine-Venetian churches, dedicated to Agios Georgios and Agia Irene. *Map E3*

5 Topolia

This village, en route from Kastelli to Paleochora, stands amid farm terraces, fields and olive groves, in a well watered

Kournas

valley which leads into Kartsomatados Gorge. Its small church of Agia Paraskevi dates from the late Byzantine era. ✥ *Map B3*

6 Elos
Elos is one of the settlements known as the Enea Choria ("Nine Villages"), which are set among the chestnut forests of the Selloni region. At 1,200 m (3,700 ft) above sea level, it can be pleasantly cooler than the south coast beaches in summer. Surrounded by woodland, Elos has a 14th-century Byzantine chapel and a ruined Turkish aqueduct. ✥ *Map B3*

7 Alikianos
A ruined Venetian castle of the aristocratic Molini family *(see p41)* and a noted 14th-century church of Agios Ioannis (or "Ai-Kir Yanni" in local Cretan dialect) are the prime sights of Alikianos. The village is picturesque in itself, however, and surrounded by citrus groves. ✥ *Map C2*

8 Hamezi
Set above the Bay of Siteia, Hamezi has been inhabited since the Minoan era. Indeed, remnants of Minoan buildings can be seen on a hilltop from the present

Voila

village, which is a peaceful clutter of whitewashed stone cottages, offset by colourful displays of flowers. ✥ *Map P5*

9 Voila
Voila is Crete's most dramatic ghost village, with lizards scuttling across its ruined walls and crumbling doorways. Voila is overlooked by the tumbledown walls of a Venetian hilltop castle and a Turkish tower, and the only building still intact is the church of Agios Giorgios. Surprisingly, two Turkish drinking fountains still provide visitors with fresh water. ✥ *Map Q5*

10 Ethia
It is hard to believe that this desolate hamlet was an important place during Venetian occupation, when it was the fief of the De Mezzo family. Their ruined family tower is now recognized as an important Venetian building, worthy of restoration. ✥ *Map Q5*

Left **Lake Kournas** Right **View from Vai**

Areas of Natural Beauty

1 White Mountains (Lefka Ori)

The White Mountain region of Crete is one of Europe's pocket wildernesses, a region of savage, desert mountains traversed by deep gorges through which small streams flow in spring. The best known of these is the lovely Samaria Gorge *(see pp26–27)*. In winter, the White Mountain peaks are under heavy snow, but in summer temperatures can rise to 35°C. ® *Map C–D4*

Windmill, Lasithi Plateau

2 Lasithi

It is still promoted to tourists as the "Plain of Windmills", but few of the thousands of white-sailed windmills exist in working order. That said, the drive to this bowl of rich farmland surrounded by mountains is stunning in itself. Lasithi's patchwork of fertile fields, gardens and orchards strikes a contrast with the treeless grey slopes surrounding it. ® *Map M4*

3 Elafonisi

This tiny islet, a stone's throw from the mainland, may in Venetian or Byzantine times have been a preserve for deer, for its name means "deer island". Between Elafonisi and the shore is a lagoon of turquoise water. It is possible to reach the island simply by wading *(see also p46)*. ® *Map A4*

4 Vai

A group of sturdy date palms on a crescent of sandy beach at Vai is claimed to be Europe's only palm forest. The palms may originally have been planted by Arab raiders or ancient Phoenicians. Today the palm grove is

The White Mountains

carefully protected.
✎ *Map R4*

Lake Votamos (Zaros)

Fed by an underground spring which provides Crete with most of its bottled mineral water, Lake Votamos is a deep blue ring of cool, clear water surrounded by

Omalos Plateau

flinty, barren slopes. Tavernas near the shore serve grilled trout from the lake, and a good gorge walk starts nearby. ✎ *Map J5*

Imbros Gorge

Not as long as the spectacular Samaria Gorge, the Imbros Gorge extends between the villages of Komitades and Imbros. Its narrowest point is only 2 m (6 ft) wide. It is a three to four hour walk. ✎ *Map D4*
• *7am–sunset* • *Adm charge in summer*

Omalos Plateau

A fertile plain, ringed by rocky slopes, lies high up on the northern side of the White Mountains. Millennia of winter rains have washed the topsoil down from the surrounding slopes to create this upland oasis. Most people pass through without stopping, but, especially in spring, this is one of the prettiest, most peaceful spots in Crete. ✎ *Map C3*

Lake Kournas

Terrapins and migrant water birds are among the wildlife to be seen in and around Crete's main body of fresh water. It is prettiest in spring and early summer. ✎ *Map E3*

Kourtaliotiko Gorge

Frogs, terrapins and tiny water snakes splash and slither in freshwater pools at the bottom of the pretty canyon which emerges near Plakias on the south coast. ✎ *Map F4*

Aspros Potamos

The valley of the "white river" – a stream which, like most Cretan watercourses, flows only in winter and spring – opens into the sea at the east end of Makrygialos beach. Surrounded by pines, boulder-covered slopes, terraced fields and olive groves, it makes a pleasant walk.
✎ *Map P5*

Left **Chapel between Agia Roumeli and Loutro** Right **Zakros Gorge**

Mountain Walks

Samaria Gorge
Passing through the ruggedly beautiful scenery of the Samaria National Park, the Samaria Gorge is Crete's most popular walk. The track descends steeply at first from the Omalos plateau, then passes through pine woods, wild flower meadows and ruined, deserted villages to emerge on the Libyan Sea at the small village of Agia Roumeli (see pp26–27).

Samaria Gorge

Across the Lefka Ori
A two-day traverse of the savage, treeless wilderness of the high White Mountains is spectacular, but only for very fit, experienced mountain walkers. The White Mountains rise to summits of almost 2,500 m (8,000 ft), and the climate is bitterly cold in winter and scorchingly hot in summer. ✪ Map C–D4
• Eos Mountain Refuge, Kallergi • 28210 44647
• Open Apr–Oct

Imbros Gorge
The gorge, which cuts through the western fringes of the White Mountains, is a slightly shorter hike than the better known and much busier Samaria Gorge, but is

almost as spectacular and – especially in spring and autumn- allows you to escape from the crowds of day visitors. ✪ Map D4

Sougia-Agia Roumeli
The walk begins in the sleepy beach village of Sougia, on the eastern fringe of the White Mountains, and climbs first through fields and pastureland, then meadows of wild flowers and pine woods, onto barren slopes high above the sea, before descending to Agia Roumeli. Astute navigational skills and a good map are required. ✪ Map C4

Agia Roumeli-Loutro
This one-day walk follows a path along the pebbly beach of Agios Pavlos, then climbs the

Loutro

Lasithi Plateau

steep "Marble Stair" onto a high, pine-wooded plateau, descends into the Aradena Gorge, and finally zig-zags down a steep cliff to the delightful holiday village of Loutro. ◈ *Map C–D4*

Zakros Gorge
6 Also known as the "Valley of the Dead", the walk through the Zakros Gorge follows a dry stream bed through eroded limestone cliffs with caves that were used as tombs by the Minoans. ◈ *Map Q5*

Climbing Mt Idi
7 The eight-hour ascent of the 2,456-m (8,055-ft) Mt Idi (also called Psiloritis), Crete's highest mountain, begins on the Nida Plateau. An arduous climb, it should be attempted only by experienced walkers. ◈ *Map G4*

Mt Kofinas
8 Allow around five hours to climb from the remote village of Kapetaniana to the summit of Kofinas and back. There are fine views of Mt Idi, the Dikti range, and the south coast. ◈ *Map J6*

Diktian Cave (Lasithi)
9 The flat, dish-shaped Lasithi Plateau offers easy walking on dirt tracks and paths through fields, olive groves and orchards. Starting from Tzermiadou, the 7-km (4-mile) stroll to the Diktian Cave takes about two hours. ◈ *Map L5*

E4 European Mountaineering Footpath
10 Only for very fit and experienced walkers, this is a long, arduous trek with poor route marking, a traverse of the island that takes at least 30 days to complete. ◈ *Mountaineering Club of Chania, Tzanakaki 90, Chania • 28210 44647*

Mount Idi

Left **Lammergeier vulture** Right **Scarce swallowtail butterfly**

TOP 10 Wildlife

1 Wild Goat

The Cretan wild goat, or *kri-kri*, is one of Europe's rarest mammals. The shy creature is found in small numbers in the Samaria Gorge National Park, in the heart of the White Mountains and on Dia Island, off Crete's north coast.

Wild goat

2 Lammergeier

The rare Lammergeier vulture, Europe's largest bird of prey, may be seen soaring high above the Omalos Plateau or in the high reaches of the White Mountains. Nicknamed the "bone-breaker", the Lammergeier feeds on the carcasses of goats and sheep, and sometimes smashes bones open by dropping them from a great height to get at the marrow.

3 Pelican

The Dalmatian pelican, which breeds in the lakes and wetlands of northern Greece, Macedonia and Albania, migrates south to the Nile Delta for the winter. A few birds sometimes make landfall in Crete after being blown off course by storms or having become exhausted by the force of strong headwinds.

4 Eleonora's Falcon

The very rare Eleonora's falcon breeds on some of Crete's offshore islands and can sometimes be seen performing its remarkable aerobatics above the steep cliffs of Zakros, in eastern Crete.

5 Cretan Spiny Mouse

The Cretan spiny mouse is unique to the island. Like most small rodents, it is nocturnal and is therefore not the easiest of the island's mammals to see. Look out for its endearingly large ears and blunt spines against rocky slopes at twilight.

6 Gecko

Big-eyed gecko lizards, with sucker-tipped fingers that enable them to cling to walls and ceilings, inhabit many older buildings, coming out after dark to hunt insects. You may see several clinging to the wall near outdoor

Dalmatian pelicans

Gecko

lamps, waiting to snap up moths and mosquitoes attracted by the light.

Scops Owl
The tiny Scops owl, with its grey plumage and bright yellow eyes, is common in Crete. It nests in holes in battered stone walls and roosts on roadside telephone poles or tree stumps. You are most likely to see Scops owls at dusk, but after dark they can often be heard calling to each other – a monotonous, one-note hoot.

Cretan Argus Butterfly
The beautiful Cretan argus butterfly is limited to the higher slopes of the Dikti and Idi mountains. This large, dark brown butterfly is increasingly endangered through loss of habitat.

Scarce Swallowtail
Europe's largest butterfly is the dramatically patterned scarce swallowtail, its pale yellow wings marked with dark zebra stripes, and red and blue eye-spots. It's a strong flyer and may be seen all over Crete in summer.

Cretan Wild Cat
Cretan shepherds have long claimed that the wilder parts of the island are home to a large wild cat called the *fourokattos*. The first live specimen of this elusive beast was caught in the mid-1990s by Italian zoologists. Weighing 5.5 kg (12 lbs), with a tawny pelt and a formidable snarl, the Cretan wild cat is unique in Europe.

Trees and Flowers

Wild Olive
The wild olive hangs on in the sheltered gorges of Crete's rocky slopes where few other trees thrive.

Cretan Ebony
Putting out spikes of pink flowers in spring, the Cretan ebony clings to steep, rocky cliffs and mountainsides.

Dragon Arum
With its foul-smelling red flower and spike, the dragon arum is a motif in several Minoan frescoes and a reality in shady spots beneath trees.

Yellow Bee Orchid
The yellow bee orchid, bearing flowers that imitate the insects it attracts, blooms profusely on mountain slopes in spring.

Catchfly
The catchfly, with its ragged bright-pink flowers, traps insects on the sap-coated hairs of its sticky stems.

Yellow Horned Poppy
This poppy lends a splash of colour to rocky stretches of the Cretan foreshore.

Giant Reed
The giant calamus reed grows as high as 4 m (13 ft) on the banks of Cretan streams.

Autumn Cyclamen
In October, flowering from apparently barren ground, the autumn cyclamen signals the end of summer.

Spring Crocus
This mauve flower with vivid yellow stamens flowers early in the year.

Evergreen Plane
Endemic to Crete, the tough evergreen plane has evolved to cope with the harsh island environment.

Crete's Top 10

Left **The defeat of Athens by King Minos** Right **Nikos Kazantzakis**

🔟 Famous Cretans

1 Zeus
Paramount among the Greek gods, Zeus was said to have been born and raised in caves *(see p58)*. His mother sheltered him from his child-devouring father, the Titan Kronos, whom Zeus eventually slew, giving rise to a new dynasty of gods.

Zeus

2 King Minos
Minos, King of Crete and both patron and tormentor of the ingenious Daedalos, appears in the Greek myths as a tyrant. In fact, the legendary Minos is probably a composite of many Minoan kings, whose power and wealth were remembered long after their civilization fell.

3 Nicephoros Phokas
The Byzantine general Nicephoros Phokas reconquered Crete from the Saracens in 961. Laying siege to their capital at Khandak (Irakleio), he demoralized the garrison by firing the heads of their captured comrades over the walls of the city.

4 Michael Damaskinos
Michailis Damaskinos (circa 1530–91) is the best known of the Cretan School icon

painters. Some of his most important works are exhibited in the Museum of Religious Art in Irakleio *(see p13)*.

5 El Greco
Born in the twilight years of Venetian rule in Crete, Domenikos Theotokopoulos (1541–1614) studied the icon painters of the Cretan School; their influence can be seen in the elongated features of his subjects and his vivid use of colour. He trained under Titian in Italy, then moved to Toledo, where he acquired his Spanish nickname of El Greco: "the Greek".

6 Vinzentzos Kornaros
This 16th-century poet (died 1677) was a contemporary of El Greco and Damaskinos and is remembered for his life's work, the Erotokritos, post-Byzantine Greece's greatest work of epic literature.

7 Nikos Kazantzakis
Born in Irakleio, Kazantzakis (1883–1957) is best known for his novel *Alexis Zorbas*, translated into English and filmed as *Zorba the Greek*. He was

El Greco

Eleftherios Venizelos

excommunicated by the Orthodox Church for his humanist views, and his self-penned epitaph reads: "I hope for nothing. I fear nothing. I am free."

8 Eleftherios Venizelos

Born at Mournies near Chania, Venizelos (1864–1936) made his reputation in the 1889 and 1896 uprisings. He led the campaign for union with Greece, and went on to become the Greek premier, dominating the nation's politics until the 1930s. He then became involved in a failed republican coup d'etat and was forced to flee the country, dying in exile in Paris.

9 Ioannis Daskalogiannis

Ioannis Daskalogiannis (died 1770) raised the clans of the mountainous and inaccessible Sfakia region in the first major rebellion against Turkey in 1770. The uprising failed, and when Daskalogiannis attempted to negotiate a surrender at Frangokastello he was seized, tortured and skinned alive – a not uncommon penalty for rebels against the sultan.

10 Chatzimichalis Dalianis

Dalianis garrisoned the fort at Frangokastello with only 385 men during the nationwide uprising in 1821. On the mainland, the rebellion succeeded, giving birth to the modern Greek state, but in Crete it failed. Dalianis and his men, overwhelmingly outnumbered by the Turks, were massacred in a valiant final stand.

Top 10 Works of Art and Literature

1 *Zorba the Greek* by Kazantzakis
The freedom-loving spirit of Greece is to the fore in this early 20th-century tragi-comedy.

2 *Erotokritos* by Vinzentzos Kornaros
Ten thousand lines of epic poetry written in the 15-syllable heptametric style of Byzantium.

3 *Travellers on the Way to the Monastery of St Catherine* by El Greco
El Greco's only painting to be seen in Crete (in the Historical Museum in Knosos).

4 *Lord, Thou Art Great* by Ioannis Kornaros
This is one of Crete's most dazzling and famous icons; it resides at Moni Toplou (p42).

5 Paintings by Lefteris Kanakakis
Rethymno's Contemporary Arts Centre houses a variety of Kanakakis's work.

6 *The Bull from the Sea* by Mary Renault
A fictional retelling of the ancient legend of Theseus, Minos and the Minotaur.

7 The Cretan Journal of Edward Lear
Lear's illustrated diary of a journey to Crete in 1864.

8 *Officers & Gentlemen* by Evelyn Waugh
A pithy account of the British in Crete in World War II.

9 *Adoration of the Magi* by Damaskinos
A portrayal of the veneration of the infant Jesus (Museum of Religious Art, Irakleio).

10 Frescoes of Moni Valsamonerou
Variously attributed to Damaskinos and 15th-century painter Konstantinos Rikos.

Crete's Top 10

Left **Hercules and his labours** Right **Theseus and Ariadne in a boat**

Myths and Legends

1 The Birth of Zeus

Zeus was the sixth child of the Titan Kronos, who had devoured his other children to prevent them from overthrowing him as he had overthrown his own father, Uranus, ruler of the old gods. Born in the Diktian Cave in Crete, Zeus was hidden by his mother Rhea and raised in the Idaian Cave on Mount Idi. Zeus eventually poisoned Kronos, making him regurgitate his siblings, who overthrew the Titans to become the new gods and goddesses.

2 Zeus and Europa

Though married to the goddess Hera, Zeus took many mortal lovers, one of whom was the princess Europa, daughter of the King of Phoenicia. Taking the form of a white bull, Zeus carried Europa off to Crete, where he took her as his wife.

3 The Minotaur and the Labyrinth

In the myth of King Minos (one of the sons of Zeus and Europa), his queen Pasiphae bore a child, half bull and half man, after coupling with the sacred bull of Zeus. Minos imprisoned this monster, the Minotaur, in a tortuous maze, the subterranean labyrinth.

Europa on the Bull

4 Theseus and Ariadne

Minos demanded tribute of youths and maidens from the Athenians after defeating them in war. The victims were given to the Minotaur, but Theseus, prince of Athens, slew the Minotaur and escaped the labyrinth with the help of Minos's daughter Ariadne, who gave him a ball of thread to retrace his steps.

5 Talos the Bronze Giant

According to myth, Zeus created the bronze giant to defend Crete. It patrolled the coasts, hurling huge boulders to sink vessels that came too close. Talos was finally slain by Jason, with the aid of the sorceress Medea, who pointed out the giant's only weak spot, a vein near its ankle.

6 Daedalus and Ikarus

Daedalus and his son, Ikarus, made wings of feathers held together with beeswax in order to escape imprisonment at the hands of King Minos – punishment for helping Theseus slay the Minotaur. Ikarus flew too high and the sun's heat melted the wax, causing him to plummet into the sea, but Daedalus reached safety in Sicily.

The death of Talos

Daedalus and Ikarus

Hercules and the Bull of Crete
The demigod Hercules, son of Zeus and the mortal woman Alkmene, was set 12 tasks by King Eurystheus of Argos, one of which was to capture and tame the untameable bull of Crete.

Nymphs of Dragolaki
The cave known as the Dragolaki or "Dragon's Lair", just outside the Sfakia mountain village of Agios Ioannis, is said to be haunted by Nereids, water-nymphs who were daughters of the god Nereus.

The Immortal Plane Tree at Gortys
Zeus ravished Europa beneath this huge plane tree near the Roman ruins of Gortys. As a result, the tree is said never to shed its leaves, even in winter.

The Drossoulites of Frangokastello
Phantoms are said to emerge on 17 May every year from the sea mists and ride into the deserted little fortress at Frangokastello (see p40). They are the ghosts of Chatzimichalis Dalianis (see p57) and his men, massacred by the Turks here in 1821.

Top 10 Caves

1 Sfendoni
Crete's most spectacular cave, crammed with strange rock formations deep beneath the Idi range.

2 Diktian Cave (Diktaion Antron)
Said to be the birthplace of Zeus, this cave above the Lasithi Plateau contains an artificial lake.

3 Idaian Cave
This enormous cavern on the slopes of Mount Idi was Zeus's childhood hideout.

4 Kamares
This cave on Mount Idi's southern face lends its name to the sophisticated Minoan pottery discovered here.

5 Skotino
This is one of Crete's largest caves. It was first dedicated to virgin goddess Britomartis and later became a sanctuary to Artemis.

6 Inatos
The goddess Ilithia, daughter of Zeus and Hera, was worshipped in this grotto, which delves into the sea-cliff above Tsoutsouros.

7 Ilithia
Archaic stone figures of pregnant women have been found in this cave, birthplace of the goddess Ilithia.

8 Profitis Ilias
Like the Diktian Cave, this cave near Arkalochori is also claimed as birthplace of Zeus.

9 Melidoni
This cave was said to be the lair of Talos, the bronze giant created by Zeus.

10 Cave of the Holy Fathers
This gloomy cave in the remote Sellino highlands is now a Greek Orthodox shrine.

Left **Musicians playing the lyra** Centre **Rural piper** Right **Dance performance**

Music and Instruments

Lyra and laouta

Lyra

The three-stringed *lyra* is typical of Crete, although the instrument is also found in mainland Greece. It is similar in shape to a violin, but has a far more rounded, pear-shaped body and the neck is stouter. The *lyra* player props the instrument on one knee and plays it with a small bow, producing melodies and harmonies that may be merry, martial or melancholy.

Laouta

The *laouta* is the Cretan version of the mandolin and is one of the most important instruments for Cretan musicians and compo-sers. It is usually used to provide a backing rhythm for the *lyra*, and like the *lyra* is an essential member of any Cretan ensemble. However, the *laouta* is sometimes also heard as a solo instrument.

Bouzouki

The eight-stringed *bouzouki* is an eastern relative of the guitar and its origins are probably in Asia Minor. *Bouzouki* music gained popularity in mainland Greece after the exchange of Greek and Turkish populations in the 1920s, but the *bouzouki* has always been in use in Crete.

Santouri

The hammer dulcimer or *santouri* is another import from Asia Minor into Greece, where it was not widely played until the 1920s, though Alexis Zorbas, hero of *Zorba the Greek*, claimed playing the *santouri* among his many talents.

Gerakokoudouna (Hawk Bells)

Cretan *lyra* players sometimes attach tiny copper or silver hawk bells to the horsehair bows with which the *lyra* is played. These little bells, as well as having an ornamental purpose, can be made to provide an occasional lively and rhythmic jingling accompaniment.

Musicians outside a local kafeneia, traditional café

The askomandoura

Diouli

6 The *diouli* is a small hand drum of wood and goatskin which in a traditional Greek music ensemble represents the entire percussion section.

Voulgari

7 The *voulgari*, a Cretan version of the long-necked lute known in Turkey as the *saz*, was a popular solo instrument in Cretan village music but is rarely heard now.

Askomandoura (Bagpipe)

8 The *askomandoura*, or Greek bagpipe, was once a popular instrument around the southern Aegean islands. Like some other seldom heard instruments, it is undergoing a minor revival as a new wave of younger musicians rediscover their musical roots.

Kithara (Guitar)

9 The guitar, whether acoustic or (more often) electric, has sadly ousted many of the older instruments and, even at village festivals, weddings and saints days, has become a standard member of the Cretan ensemble.

Baglamas

10 Not unique to Crete, this stringed instrument was the poor man's makeshift *bouzouki*, home-made with a dried gourd or sometimes a tortoiseshell for a sound box and wire strings.

Top 10 Traditional Songs and Dances

1 Haniotis
The *haniotis* is a dignified line dance for men and women that comes from Chania.

2 Pidiktos
The *pidiktos*, a dance from eastern Crete, involves great athletic leaps and bounds.

3 Pentozalis
The *pentozalis's* sprightly rhythms are reminiscent of the jigs and reels of Irish and Scottish folk music.

4 Sousta
A flirtatious dance for the young, and a favourite at weddings and festivals.

5 Hasapikos ("Zorba's Dance")
The *hasapikos* or "butcher's dance" provided inspiration for "Zorba's Dance" in the film *Zorba the Greek*.

6 Siganos
The dignified *siganos* for groups of men and woman is a dance for any festival.

7 Mandinades
The traditional rhyming couplets – usually love songs – are typical of Crete's rich oral tradition, which comes to the fore in local festivals.

8 Rizitiko
The *rizitiko* is Crete's warrior dance, in which male performers act out scenes of combat and heroism.

9 Syrtos
Performed all over Greece, the *syrtos* is the best known of the Greek circle dances.

10 Rembetika
The Greek version of the urban blues, brought to Greece by refugees from Asia Minor in the 1920s, is popular with young Cretans.

Left **Traditional Greek dancing** Right **Lighting candles for the Virgin Mary**

Festivals and Events

An Easter meal with bread and dyed eggs

Easter
This is the most important celebration of the Greek year. It is predominantly a family affair, focusing on the home, where spit-roasted goat is the highlight of a day of eating and drinking. More formal, religious processions are led by fabulously attired priests or monks and are often followed by fireworks. In many towns and villages Easter culminates with the burning of an effigy of Judas Iscariot.

Moni Arkadiou

Festival of the Virgin Mary, 15 Aug
The Festival of the Virgin Mary (*Apokimisis tis Panayias*) is second only to Easter and tends to be a much more public celebration. Church processions are followed by open-air eating and drinking in the churchyard or village square, in turn followed by music and dancing until the early hours.

Arkadiou, 7–9 Nov
A patriotic three-day gathering to commemorate the freedom fighters of the 1866 uprising and the defenders of Moni Arkadiou, who blew themselves up rather than surrender to the Turks.

Sultanina, Siteia, first two weeks Aug
Siteia's sultana festival is a relaxed celebration of the grape harvest, with music, dancing, lashings of local wine and nightly performances in the old Venetian fortress, now restored as an open air theatre.

Chestnut Festival, mid-Oct
This festival of the chestnut harvest is most fervently celebrated in the village of Elos in southwest Crete. Music, dancing, eating and drinking all play their part.

Festival of St Nicholas, Agios Nikolaos, 6 Dec
Many processions and celebrations abound at Agios Nikolaos to celebrate the town's patron saint, who is also venerated all over the island.

Roasting goat on the spit at Easter

Epiphany, 6 Jan

In the Greek calendar, Epiphany ends the 12-day reign of mischievous spirits who run loose during

Diving at Epiphany

Christmas. Ceremonial rites banish the spirits until the next year, and baptismal fonts, springs and wells are blessed by local priests or monks. In some places such as Chora Sfakion, young men dive for a crucifix tossed into the harbour by a priest.

Independence Day/Feast of the Annunciation, 25 Mar

A national festival commemorating the beginning of Greece's final struggle for independence in 1821. It is combined with the celebration of the Feast of the Annunciation, and so religious processions are followed by military parades in major towns, along with music and dancing all the way.

St George's Day, 23 Apr

At the Church of Asi Gonia Apokoronou near Rethymno, hundreds of Cretan shepherds bring their sheep to be blessed on St George's Day each year, hoping to ensure healthy flocks and a prosperous year. In return, the shepherds distribute free sheep's milk.

Festival of Agios Titos, 25 Aug

The biggest celebration to mark the day of Crete's patron saint is at Irakleio, where icons and relics are carried through the streets with great pomp. The saint's day is also celebrated at churches across the island.

Top 10 Saints

1 Agios Titos (St Titus)
This follower of St Paul was given the task of bringing Christianity to the Cretans.

2 Agios Nikolaos (St Nicholas)
The patron saint of seafarers and fishermen is honoured all around the coast of Crete.

3 Agios Pavlos (St Paul)
The chapel of Agios Pavlos stands where the saint was swept ashore between Agia Roumeli and Loutro.

4 Agios Michalis (St Michael)
The commander of the heavenly host is especially revered by combative Cretans.

5 Agios Giorgios (St George)
The patron saint of shepherds is greatly esteemed and, as a warrior saint, is doubly popular.

6 Agios Eftihios (St Eustacius)
St Eustacius is especially popular in southwest Crete, where many chapels and children bear his name.

7 Ag. Ioannis Theologos (St John the Divine)
St John wrote the *Book of Revelations* on Patmos, but he is also venerated on Crete.

8 Profitis Ilias (Prophet Elijah)
Many mountain-top chapels for this prophet may originally have been for the sun-god Helios.

9 Agioi Deka (Ten Saints)
Ten Cretan martyrs killed for their faith by the Romans have their church near Gortys.

10 Ag. Ioannis Prodromos (St John the Baptist)
St John is often shown in Greek art wearing goat-skin breeches, like the pre-Christian god Pan.

Crete's Top 10

Left **Odos Souliou, Rethymno** Centre **Odos Daedalou, Irakleio** Right **Odos Dimitrakaki**

TOP 10 Markets and Shopping Streets

1 Chania Market, Plateia Venizelou, Chania

The market building is a Chania landmark and bustles with vendors and shoppers. A visual feast and also the place to buy herbs, olive oil, dried fruit, honey and typical Cretan souvenirs, such as the tiny metal pots used to brew Greek coffee. ✆ *Map D2/B6*

Odos Skridlof, Chania

2 Odos Skridlof, Chania

Running through the centre of the old quarter, this has been a street of saddlemakers and cobblers for centuries, perhaps even millennia. These days, satchels, sandals and handbags abound. ✆ *Map D2/B6*

3 Boutari Winery, Archanes

The best wines in Crete (and from other parts of Greece) can be tasted and bought in this new visitor centre at Crete's top winery on the Fantaxommetocho vineyard *(see also p81)*. ✆ *70100 Archanes • 2810 731617 • Map K4*

4 Odos 1866, Irakleio

Irakleio's main market street and a great place to shop for Cretan herbs and tisanes. It also offers an insight into the Cretan diet – along with the olives, you will see buckets of live snails for sale. ✆ *Map K3*

5 Odos Daedalou, Irakleio

Named after the legendary inventor of the Labyrinth *(see p58)*, this road is rather more up-market than Odos 1866, and is lined with shops selling jewellery and linen and cotton clothes to summer visitors. ✆ *Map K3*

6 Museum Shops

For quality replicas of finds from the archaeological sites of Crete, visit the Museum Shops, in the former Venetian Loggia on Odos Paleologou in Rethymno and in the Byzantine Museum in Chania. ✆ *Map Q2 & A5*

7 Local Products Exhibition, Farmers' Union of Siteia

Promoting the produce of local farmers, this co-operative venture is well worth visiting just to see how the vines and olives of Crete are grown and processed. It is also a good place for quality olive oil, wine and raki, Crete's favourite spirit. ✆ *Map Q4 • Open by appt: 69471 67700*

Souvenir shop, Irakleio

8 Odos Souliou, Rethymno

Rethymno's up-market shopping street, lined with stores selling copies of Minoan pottery, traditional Cretan pottery and modern ceramics, as well as colourful cotton and linen, lace and embroidery. ✎ *Map F3/Q2*

9 Odos Ethnikis Andistasi, Rethymno

The most photogenic market in Crete spills out – as indeed it has for centuries – from open-fronted shops and stalls along Odos Ethnikis Andistasi and around the Venetian Porta Guora. Go early in the morning, when it is in full cry and waiters bustle from stall to stall with coffee and raki. ✎ *Map F3/Q2*

10 New Marina, Rethymno

An open-air market takes place every Thursday morning from 7am until 1pm. Stalls sell local produce, fruit and vegetables, cheese, honey, flowers and clothing. There is also a smaller market on Saturday mornings in the square next to the bus station. ✎ *Map F3*

Porta Guora, Rethymno

Top 10 Traditional Shops

1 Xilouris Popular Art, Anogeia

The ancient art of handloom weaving. ✎ *Milopotamou*

2 Cretan Handicraft, Mirthios

Vividly coloured weavings, shepherds' sticks, embroidery, lace, herbs, wines, raki and olive oil. ✎ *74060 Mirthios*

3 To Maxairadiko, Chania

The best of a clutch of traditional knifemakers on the street. ✎ *18 Sifakas*

4 Voskakis Workshop, Amari Valley

Nikos Voskakis hand-carves olive wood platters, bowls, dishes, candle sticks and cutlery. ✎ *Blzari*

5 Nikos Siragas, Rethymno

Artistic wood-turner acquiring an international reputation for his beautiful handmade bowls, vases and works of art. ✎ *Petalioti 2, Rethymno*

6 Landen Apan, Chania

Traditional foodstuffs of Crete. ✎ *Daskalogianni 70*

7 Ypsanta Selinou, Paleochora

Tiny shop on a nameless lane, with tapestries, rugs and lace. ✎ *Off main street*

8 Top Hanas, Chania

Wonderful stock of old Cretan rugs, blankets and kilims. ✎ *3 Angelou*

9 Roka Carpets, Chania

Cretan textile weaving. ✎ *Zambeliou 61*

10 Komboloi 52, Chania

Old-fashioned rosaries made from olive wood, amber, jet, turquoise etc. ✎ *Dimotiki Agora 52*

Left **Dining in a traditional taverna** Centre **Greek coffee** Right **Octopuses hanging out to dry**

🔟 Food and Drink

1 Tsikoudia

Tsikoudia or *raki* (like Italian grappa) is a colourless spirit distilled from the skins and stems left after grape pressing. You may see market traders starting the day with a shot of *tsikoudia* and a strong coffee. It is also drunk after meals.

Tsikoudia, strong spirit

2 Retsina

Retsina is a white wine flavoured with pine resin. The flavour was originally imparted by the pine storage barrels, but today the resin is added before bottling. It is often served chilled, though locally made *retsina* may be available from the barrel *(apo to bareli)*, traditionally being served in copper jugs.

3 Wines

Cretan wines are becoming more sophisticated as makers introduce techniques pioneered by New World producers. The Boutari company's Fantaxometocho vineyard at Archanes *(see p81)*, where award-winning white wines are made, offers a guided tour, tasting opportunities and a shop.

4 Olives

Olives and Greece are inseparable. Indeed, without the olive – which has provided not only food but also oil for lamps, wood for fuel and timber for building ships and homes – Crete might not have become the cradle of Minoan civilization. Olives are sold in a bewildering array of sizes and flavours, with as many as 40 different types available from all over Greece.

5 Cheeses (Staka and Mizithra)

Far more delicious than the ubiquitous feta are Crete's own cheeses, such as *mizithra*, made from fresh sheep's milk, and *staka*, made from whey.

6 Cretan Sausages (Loukanika)

Loukanika – small spicy pork sausages – are found all over Greece, but those from Crete are reckoned to be among the best. They may be served fried *(tiganita)* or smoked *(kapnista)*, and are a regular feature of a lavish meze (dish of appetizers).

Left **Green and black olives** Right **Cretan cheeses**

Loukanika, the spicy Cretan sausages

7 Greek Coffee (Kafe Elliniko)
Finely ground coffee and sugar are boiled together in small metal pots to make a thick, black drink, which is served in a tiny cup along with a tall glass of water. To order a sweet coffee, ask for *glykou*; for medium-sweet, ask for *metriou*; and for coffee without sugar order *skieto*.

8 Snails (Saligkaria)
Once a valuable source of protein in hard times, snails are now regarded as a delicacy. *Saligkaria stifado* (snail casserole) is a uniquely Cretan dish, and is unlikely to be found on the menu in tourist restaurants.

9 Soup (Kreatosoupa and Patsa)
Cretan peasant cooking makes full use of any animal slaughtered. *Kreatosoupa* (meat soup) is made from the bones and left-over scraps of goat, mutton or beef, while *patsa* is a rich soup made with tripe. Both are often served at festivals, when a goat is traditionally slaughtered and spit-roasted as a family meal.

10 Octopus
Octopus *(oktapodi)* are caught by spear fishing, tenderized by pounding on a rock, then hung to dry in the sun before being grilled over charcoal or cooked in a casserole *(stifado)* with onions and cumin.

Herbs

1 Dittany
Taking its name from the Dikti mountains, this variety of oregano is unique to Crete and has long been credited with restorative powers.

2 Sage
Sage from the Cretan mountains is a favourite medicinal *tisane*, and is said to cure fever, chills, sore throats and rheumatism.

3 Saffron
Deriving from the crocus flower, costly saffron is used sparingly to add colour and flavour to soups and stews.

4 Thyme
Sweet-scented thyme, with its deep purple flowers, grows wild on Crete's roadsides and hillsides.

5 Coriander
Coriander is used fresh as a flavouring and garnish for stews, grills and salads.

6 Cinnamon
Cretans acquired a taste for spices during the Turkish and Venetian trading eras. Today, cinnamon flavours desserts like *rizokalo* (rice pudding) and sweet pies.

7 Cumin
Another exotic import, cumin is essential in the slowly cooked casserole *stifado*.

8 Rosemary
Growing in abundance, rosemary is used by Cretans mainly to flavour fish dishes.

9 Mint
This ubiquitous wild herb scents the air on rural walks and flavours dozens of dishes.

10 Fennel
Growing profusely in the countryside, this member of the aniseed family is used to flavour ouzo, the national drink.

Crete's Top 10

Left **Giovanni, Irakleio** Centre **Karnagio, Chania** Right **Veneto, Rethymno**

Restaurants

Tamam, Chania
Popular with Chania's locals as well as holidaymakers, Tamam has a menu that takes in cuisine from right around the shores of the Eastern Mediterranean. Good choice for vegetarians too *(see p101)*.

Ela, Chania
One of Chania's most popular restaurants, set within the ruins of a Venetian mansion. The menu is wide in scope, combining traditional Greek dishes with international favourites, as well as a few more authentically Cretan offerings *(see p101)*.

Amphissa olives

Kariatis, Chania
An imaginative menu at this fine Italian restaurant in the eastern harbour provides some unusual choices as well as reliable favourites such as pizza and *lasagna al forno* baked in a wood-fired oven. Elegant decor and attentive service *(see p101)*.

Karnagio, Chania
Set on Chania's Venetian harbour is Karnagio. It offers a good range of traditional dishes, as well as grilled chicken, pork and lamb, huge peasant salads and a slender range of fish dishes. All meals are substantial *(see p101)*.

Avli, Rethymno
This elegant courtyard restaurant is, arguably, the best in Rethymno. A pretty garden provides the setting for the traditional grilled and roasted meat dishes, served alongside traditional Cretan favourites such as *apatzia* (smoked sausages) and roast goat *(see p101)*.

Veneto, Rethymno
The 13th-century vaults that house the Veneto once contained a refectory for monks living in the cells above. The Veneto's menu features a number of Cretan specialities, and service is excellent *(see p101)*.

Kyria Maria, Rethymno
A friendly little taverna on a quiet alley in Rethymno's old town, near the famous Rimondi fountain. Kyria Maria serves village style dishes and is usually

Courtyard at Avli, Rethymno

Crete's Top 10

68

Recommend your favourite restaurant on **traveldk.com**

Kyria Maria, Rethymno

bustling in the evenings but quieter at lunchtime *(see p101)*.

8 Giovanni, Irakleio
The most sophisticated restaurant in Crete's capital city. As its name implies, Giovanni serves Italian dishes, plus an array of Cretan treats and re-invented traditional Greek dishes *(see p89)*.

9 The Old Mill, Elounda
The most luxurious dining on the Elounda Peninsula is in the gourmet restaurant of the Elounda Mare hotel *(see p126)*. The menu is fabulous, combining the best of Greek cooking with world-class cuisine, and dining is accompanied by piano music. There are only 20 covers, so booking well ahead is essential. Dress code formal *(see p113)*.

10 Porfira, Makrygialos
Porfira brings Cretan cooking to gourmet heights, serving a selection of uniquely Cretan dishes. The waiters are happy to guide you through the menu and will gladly explain some of the less recognizable ingredients. Set on a terrace overlooking the beach *(see p113)*.

Top 10 Fish Served in Cretan Restaurants

1 Fagri
Red sea bream, prized for its delicate white flesh, is grilled and served whole and is one of the most expensive fish dishes on the menu.

2 Melanourgia
A large, silver-scaled fish with tasty white flesh; it's usually grilled.

3 Barbounia
Small red mullet appear on almost every tourist menu, pan-fried or grilled. Each fish provides only a few delicious mouthfuls – beware of bones!

4 Marides
Tiny whitebait are dipped in flour and shallow-fried, then served with shredded lettuce and a slice of lemon.

5 Lavraki
Sea bass is baked in olive oil, red wine vinegar and rosemary, served whole.

6 Sardelles
Sardines are often wrapped in vine leaves to seal in flavour and moisture, then grilled. Salted and pickled sardines are often served as meze.

7 Xifias
Swordfish keeps its flavour well when frozen, so is a favourite with restaurateurs.

8 Skorpios
The evil-looking scorpion fish is surprisingly tasty and essential in fish soup.

9 Tonnos
Tuna steaks are best savoured in spring and autumn, when tuna migrate through Cretan waters.

10 Gopes
Nondescript-looking, bony little fish that's the cheapest on the menu, but delicious once the bones are removed.

For more restaurants around Crete **See pp89, 101 & 113**

Left **Fresh fish** Centre **Taverna Auoas, Agios Nikolaos** Right **Vegetables ripening in the sun**

Tavernas

1 Sterna tou Blou-mosifi, Vamos

Key part of a restored 19th-century stone village. The taverna serves a wide menu of Cretan specialities, baked in wood-burning ovens, and is open for breakfast, lunch and dinner *(see p101)*.

Taverna habitués

to eat in the Cherson-isos resort area. The house speciality is tender lamb *kleftiko*, roasted slowly in a paper wrapping with garlic, lemon and herbs.
⊗ *Archaiou Theatrou*
• *Map L3* • *Closed Nov–Apr* • *€€€*

2 Ta Douliana, Douliana

A typical village taverna, set in the centre of tiny Douliana. Its rickety wooden tables and chairs are on a terrace shaded by vines, and the menu focuses on hearty fare such as *arni avgolemono* (lamb with lemon sauce). ⊗ *Centre of Douliana, on road between Kalive and Vamos* • *28250 23380* • *Map E3* • *€€*

4 To Farangi, Agia Roumeli

This family-run taverna is the best place to eat in Agia Roumeli *(see pp26–7)* and serves *sfakanies pites* (pies topped with honey, a regional speciality), stuffed vegetables and vine leaves, grilled meat dishes and fish. ⊗ *Centre of Agia Roumeli* • *Map C4* • *Closed Oct–May* • *€€€*

3 Kavouri, Limin Chersonisos

Kavouri is one of the best places

5 Zorbas, Siteia

This big, old-fashioned taverna beside the harbour has not changed its traditional menu in decades. It serves meze as well as heartier meals, including mousakas and a range of grilled fish dishes *(see p113)*.

Sterna tou Bloumosifi, Vamos

6 Taverna tou Zissi, Rethymno

Zissi looks rather unprepossessing at first, housed in a drab concrete

Zorbas, Siteia

building. But inside, it serves some of the best food around. The charcoal-grilled lamb alone is worth a trip from Rethymno *(see p101).*

Marilena, Elounda

Marilena's menu concentrates on seafood, simply grilled and very fresh, and prices are not exorbitant by the standards of Elounda, which is generally the priciest place on Crete. Other Greek dishes have been adapted for foreign palates by using a little less oil *(see p113).*

Vareladika, Irakleio

A pleasant, stylish and reasonably priced eating place close to the Venetian harbour. Vareladika has a tiny outdoor terrace where you can sample the wide menu of Cretan specialities, with wine served in copper jugs from the barrel.
Ⓢ *Moni Agarathou 13 • Map K3 • €€*

Taverna Auoas, Agios Nikolaos

Handily located close to the Archaeological Museum, this taverna serves a wide variety of well-prepared traditional Cretan dishes. Ⓢ *Paleologou 44 • Map N4 • Closed Nov–Apr • €€€*

Itanos, Agios Nikolaos

In a lane just off the main square, Itanos claims to be the resort's only authentic taverna – a claim that looks increasingly shaky as tourism continues to grow. Nevertheless, the taverna serves good, affordable Cretan meals and wine, and is always busy. Ⓢ *Plateia Venizelou • Map N4 • €€€*

Top 10 Cretan Wines

1 Domaine Fantaxometocho
Excellent red wine made from Mantilaria and Kotsifali grapes. Good with lamb or chicken.

2 Chardonnay Boutari
Dry, white varietal wine – great with seafood and cheese.

3 Sauvignon Blanc Boutari
Dry white, ideal with vegetable dishes, cheeses and cold cuts.

4 Sant'Antonio
Produced from Kotsifali and Mantilaria grapes in the Peza region of central Crete by Miliarakis Brothers, this deep red wine is barrel-aged for five to six years.

5 Kokolakis
Ioannis Kokolakis bottles wines made from liatiko grapes grown in the Agrilos vineyards, not far from Siteia, which produce a light, dry red wine.

6 Kissamos
This potent red wine with a 13 per cent alcohol content comes from Romeiko grapes grown in Crete's north west.

7 Rodolino
Made from liatiko red wine grapes blended with white varieties, this rosé is best served chilled to the bone.

8 Clos de Creta
Unassuming white wine made from Romeiko grapes from the Kissamos area.

9 Domenico
Made from Vilana and Rozaki grapes, this is one of the better pine-flavoured retsinas.

10 Malvasia
One of Europe's oldest wines, Malvasia was exported as far as England by the Venetians. Made from a blend of sugar-rich, aromatic grapes, it is best drunk with dessert.

 For more places to eat and drink in Crete **See pp68–9, 72–3, 88–9, 100–101, 112–113**

Left **Fortezza, Chania** Right **Pallas Café, Chania**

🔟 Cafés and Ouzeries

Aroma, Chania

1 Pagopoieion, Irakleio
A remarkable café-bar set in the city's old icehouse, serving Italian, Greek and iced coffee all day long. The decoration includes mementos of the building's past, including the old ice lift. ◈ *Platia Ayios Titos • Map K3*

2 Aroma, Chania
With tables on the east side of the harbour, Aroma is a popular rendezvous for young locals. Fine views of the harbour and a pleasant place for breakfast, morning coffee, an aperitif or after-dinner drinks. ◈ *Akti Tombazi 4 • Map D2/B5*

3 Fortetza, Chania
Delightful café-bar midway along the mole that encloses the Venetian harbour. The best place in town for a sunset drink, with views across the water to the old town. ◈ *Palaio Limani • Map D2/B4*

4 Pallas Café, Chania
This elegant rendezvous in an old Venetian mansion on the harbour opens early and stays open late. It has tables on the quay, up on a roof terrace and inside, within rooms prettily decorated with frescoes. ◈ *Akti Tompazi 17, Old Harbour • Map D2*

5 Apicorno Café, Kalives
An attractive modern café with large indoor and outdoor seating areas. The outside tables provide a scenic view across the Bay of Souda. The café is open all day until late throughout the year and serves a variety of coffee, ice-cream and alcoholic drinks as well as a choice of breakfasts and snacks. ◈ *Main Street • Map E2*

6 Barko Café, Agios Nikolaos
Right on the seafront at Kitroplateia, this café and restaurant is a popular choice for mezes, snacks and drinks. Casual by day, it attracts the smart set in the evening. ◈ *Kitroplateia Beach • Map N4*

Pagopoieion café-bar, Irakleio

Recommend your favourite café on **traveldk.com**

Typical rural Cretan café

Meze Dishes

1 Octopus (Oktapodi)
A favourite accompaniment to a glass of ouzo, raki or retsina is a dish of octopus chunks, cooked in oil, herbs and vinegar, and served cold.

2 Marides
Tiny whitebait are coated in flour, flash-fried and served with a slice of lemon as a snack or a first course.

3 Loukanika
These smoked and spiced pork sausages are a typically Cretan snack, served more often in winter.

4 Baked Potatoes
Another typical winter snack served in mountain village ouzeries, often cooked in a wood-burning stove in the middle of the café.

5 Saganaki
A salty and aromatic cheese-based appetizer served fried or grilled as a meze dish.

6 Karpousi
Sweet and refreshing pink cubes of chilled watermelon are among the most popular summertime meze.

7 Olives
You will see more than 40 different kinds of olive for sale in Greek markets. Their strong flavours complement a glass of retsina wonderfully.

8 Gigantes
A more substantial dish: large white beans simmered in oil, herbs and tomatoes. Served cold in summer.

9 Spanakopites
Tiny spinach pies made with flaky filo pastry.

10 Melitzanosalata
A delicious savoury dip made by pureeing grilled aubergines with herbs, usually served with crusty bread.

7 To Ellinikon, Rethymno
A clutch of cafés and bars are crammed cheek by jowl into Petihaki, among them this ouzeri which serves tasty snacks, and raki and ouzo for those who have acquired a taste for Cretan-style spirits. ❧ Petihaki • Map F3/Q2

8 To Araxovoli, Rethymno
This ouzeri-restaurant next to Rethymno's Town Hall is more authentically Cretan than most, serving good mezes and fish dishes, as well as a plethora of drinks, including, of course, a choice of rakis and ouzos. Often live traditional music at night.
❧ 34 Iroon Polytehniou • Map F3

9 Anna Bei 1900, Ierapetra
As well as a proper restaurant, his all-purpose nightspot also has a traditional café and ouzo bar, serving meze in the courtyard of an attractively restored old building (see p112).

10 Kali Kardia, Siteia
Frequented more by locals than visitors, Kali Kardia ("Good Heart") makes few concessions to tourist tastes. Authentic meze, from local cheeses to grilled snails, are washed down with strong Cretan retsina straight from the barrel. ❧ Foundalidou 28 • Map Q4

For more places to eat and drink in Crete
See pp68–9, 70–71, 88–9, 100–101, 112–113

Left **Buzzing bars, Chersonisos** Right **Tavernas, Agia Galini**

🔟 Nightlife

1 Chersonisos

If you're a summer party animal, Chersonisos is the place for you. Not far from the airport, this former fishing village has become a continuous strip of bars, clubs, restaurants and guesthouses stretching along one of Crete's best beaches. A multinational (but mainly British) clientele *(see also p86)*. ✎ Map L3

New York Bar, Hersonisos

2 Malia

Malia rivals its neighbour Chersonisos as a nightlife hot spot. It has been a party town for some 30 years, and its main street is lined with cocktail bars, restaurants, video bars and dance clubs. Along this stretch, happy hour can last most of the evening *(see also p86)*. ✎ Map M4

3 Platanias

Platanias is where most of Chania's younger residents go to party on summer weekends.

There are at least a dozen great clubs, most with open-air dance floors, and things do not really start to get lively until well after midnight *(see also p98)*. ✎ Map C

4 Paleochora

A hippy hideout well into the 1980s *(see p92)*, Paleochora's nightlife is still laid-back to a fault. A handful of relaxed – and none too noisy – music bars are scattered along the Pebble Beach waterfront, where, just out of town, there are a couple of open-air discos. ✎ Map B

5 Agios Nikolaos

Agios Nikolaos has a surprisingly lively after-dark scene, compared with its day-time placidity. The town's nightlife hot spot is Odos 25 Martiou (running uphill from the southeast corner of the harbour), where there are half a dozen or more music bars with as many again around the harbour. The town's dance club scene is more limited, with only one or two full-on clubs *(see also p103)*. ✎ Map N4

6 Rethymno

Most of the liveliest music-bars are in the streets inland

Café Zargos, Agios Nikolaos

rom the harbour.
Later on, the
nightlife scene
shifts to the open-
air discos and clubs
in the resort area,
along the seafront
east of the centre
(see also pp22–3).
◈ Map F3

Nightlife on Venizelou, central Siteia

7 Irakleio
Not many
holidaymakers stay
in Crete's capital (see pp12–13),
so its nightlife scene is more
staid than in the resorts. Young
locals congregate in the cafés
and music bars around Plateia
Venizelou and Odos Chandakou,
but the discos near the harbour
are rather seedy. ◈ Map K3

8 Chania
Music blasts out from most
of the cafés and bars along the
harbour front at Chania in the
summer, and if you prefer an
evening of bar-hopping and café-
crawling to a night in the dance

Chania's harbour front at night

clubs there are few better places
in the whole of Crete. Most
younger Chaniots, however,
desert the cafés for the clubs
of Platanias after the toll of
midnight (see also pp18–19). ◈
Map D2

9 Agia, Galini
A small resort (see p86) that
has made catering to the party
crowd its specialism. Things get
lively by 11pm in a cluster of
bars and dance clubs around the
harbour, where you can club-hop
until the early hours. ◈ Map G5

10 Siteia
The nightlife is a good deal
less frenzied here than at other
resorts along the north coast,
but many a pleasant evening can
be spent wandering from bar to
bar along the waterfront. There
are half a dozen good dance
clubs (see also p103). ◈ Map Q4

AROUND THE ISLAND

Central Crete
78–89

Western Crete
90–101

Eastern Crete
102–113

CRETE'S TOP 10

Left **Malia at sunrise** Centre **Café, Irakleio market** Right **Agia Galini harbour**

Central Crete

THE LANDSCAPES OF CENTRAL CRETE *include some of the island's best beaches, rolling farmland where vines and olives flourish, and rugged mountains – among them, Crete's highest summit, Mt Idi, or Psiloritis. This was the heartland of Minoan civilization, and the most important Minoan ruins lie just south of the island's modern capital, Irakleio. Along the north coast are some busy holiday resorts, while on the south coast there are quieter, smaller places to enjoy a beach holiday in the sun.*

🔟 Sights in Central Crete

1 Ancient Knosos
2 Phaestos
3 Gortys
4 Irakleio
5 Diktian Cave
6 Lasithi
7 Mt Idi
8 Kaszantzakis Museum
9 Agia Triada
10 Boutari Winery and Audio-Visual Show

Traditional Cretan gateway, Chersonisos

Previous pages **Preveli beach**

South propylon, Knosos

Ancient Knosos

1 Knosos was pinpointed as an important archaeological site by the great Heinrich Schliemann and unearthed by British arch-aeologist Arthur Evans less than 100 years ago. The columns, courtyards and coloured frescoes of this ancient Minoan palace still have the power to amaze. Knosos was lost to history after the cataclysmic volcanic eruption that destroyed the Minoan civilization, but the site is now one of the most impressive relics of the vanished world of the Minoans *(see pp8–11)*.

Phaestos

2 This labyrinth of ruins dating from around 1600 BC includes a Minoan courtyard and theatre with tiers of stone seats, a monumental stairway, peristyle hall and a vast central courtyard. The still undeci-phered Phaestos Disc, which was discovered here, is on display in the Irakleio Archaeol-ogical Museum *(see p14)*. Phaestos was destroyed around 1450 BC by the cataclysm that also laid low the rest of Crete's Minoan palaces. Not usually as crowded as the more famous Knosos, the site at Phaestos has an impressive location on a hillside above fertile farmland *(see pp20–21)*.

The praetorium, Gortys

Gortys

3 Toppled Roman columns, a ruined Byzantine basilica, post-Minoan fortifications, and an agora, acropolis and remains of temples to Athena and Apollo all hint at the past glories of this large and little-visited arch-aeological site close to Crete's south coast. First settled in Minoan times, it became one of the most important cities of Doric Crete. It later allied itself with the Romans to become an important provincial capital, and was one of Crete's most prosperous cities until it was sacked by Arab invaders during the anarchic years of the 8th century AD *(see pp24–25)*.

Phaestos

Irakleio harbour

Irakleio
The modern capital of Crete was badly damaged in World War II, and few of its old Venetian buildings survived the reconstruction of the city. However, its Venetian fortress, harbour, arsenal and city walls are still impressive. For a morning's itinerary see pages 82–3. The city's main attraction is the Irakleio Archaeological Museum (see pp12–15).

Diktian Cave
According to ancient Greek myths, this mossy cavern, filled with strange limestone formations, was the birthplace of the greatest Olympian god, Zeus. Rhea, Zeus's mother, supposedly hid the young godling from his father, Kronos, here. Bronze figurines and Minoan double axes found in the cave are on show in the Irakleio Archaeological Museum. The site is also often referred to as the Idaian Cave. ✪ Map L5

Lasithi
The so-called "Plain of Windmills" is a high plain of fertile farmland surrounded by bare grey limestone hills. Its nickname is misleading, though. Only a few rusting metal derricks remain of the famed

Ruin, Lasithi

white-sailed windmills that once dotted the plateau in their hundreds. However, Lasithi is still worth a visit for the spectacular drive through the mountains and the glimpses it offers of a traditional way of life. ✪ Map M4

The Knosos Enigma?
Most archaeologists accept Sir Arthur Evans' view that the enigmatic maze of ruins at Knosos was a bustling hub of the greatest empire that the islands of the Aegean had ever seen. But a few "heretical" archaeologists now claim that Knosos may actually have been a giant necropolis where kings and nobles were interred, as in the tombs of ancient Egypt. The debate continues.

Mt Idi
At 2,456 m (8,055 ft), Mt Idi, which is also known as Mt Ida and Mt Psiloritis, is Crete's highest mountain. Only fit, experienced and well-equipped mountain walkers should try the eighthour hike to its summit and back. However, it is possible to drive as far as the Nida Plateau, 1,400 m (4,600 ft) above sea level, from which there are spectacular views. ✪ Map G–H4

8 Kazantzakis Museum

Cretan author Nikos Kazantzakis (1883–1957) is best known outside Greece for the novel *Alexis Zorbas*, which is set in Crete during the early 20th century. The book was filmed in 1964 as *Zorba the Greek*, starring Anthony Quinn in the title role. Kazantzakis' outspoken humanism led the Orthodox church to regard him as a heretic. The author was born in Mirtia, and a small museum in the village (in the Kazantzakis family home) is crammed with his manuscripts and diaries, film posters, photos and other memorabilia. ◉ *Map K4 • Mirtia village square, signposted • Apr–Oct: 9am–7pm daily; Nov–Mar: 10am–3pm Sun • Adm*

9 Agia Triada

Excavated by Italian archaeologists at the beginning of the 20th century, Agia Triada is smaller than other Minoan sites such as Knosos and Phaestos and was probably an aristocratic villa or a royal summer palace. Some of the finest Minoan pottery, including three carved stone vases, was discovered here and is displayed in the Irakleio Archaeological Museum. Agia Triada is only 3 km (2 miles) west of Phaestos, so can easily

Agia Triada

be visited on the same day. Because Agia Triada receives fewer vistors than the larger sites, you can explore its honeycomb of stone corridors, stairs and courtyards at your own pace. ◉ *Map G5 • 8:30am–3pm • Adm*

10 Boutari Winery and Audio-Visual Show

At the Fantaxometochi Winery, south of Knosos near Archanes village, one of Greece's leading winemakers has opened a state-of-the-art audiovisual show celebrating the island – its landscapes, history and traditional way of life. The show also highlights the vineyards and grape varieties that produce some of the Boutari family's award-winning wines. You can sample and buy Boutari red and white wines at the winery shop. ◉ *Map K4 • Apr–Oct: 9am–6pm daily; Nov–Mar: 8:30am–4:30pm daily • 28107 31617 • Adm*

The lower slopes of Mt Idi

Left **The harbour** Right **The Venetian Arsenal**

TOP 10 A Morning in Irakleio

1 Porta Kenouria
The most appropriate place to start exploring Irakleio's Venetian heritage is this ornate archway through the city's mighty walls, built in the mid-16th century by the Italian military engineer Michele Sanmichele. At this point, the walls are some 40 m (130 ft) thick, so it is not surprising that they withstood 16th-century Ottoman artillery and everything else thrown at them.

2 Pumphouse and Fountain
Walk through the portal and along Evans, named after the excavator of ancient Knosos, to Plateia Kornarou, named after the writer of the Cretan epic poem the *Erotokritos*. In the middle of this square stands a pretty, six-sided stone building, a café set within a pumphouse built by the Turks. Stop here, if you like, for a coffee in the shade of plane trees. Beside the café is the Venetian Bembo Fountain – note the broken, decapitated marble torso of a Roman statue built into its stonework.

Market stalls, Odos 1866

3 Market
Leave Plateia Kornarou north of the fountain, along the market street Odos 1866, among stalls selling fresh fruit, olives, dried fruit and nuts, and less familiar produce such as buckets of live snails. Midway along 1866, turn left and walk along to Plateia Ekaterinis, where the main landmark is the pompous 19th-century cathedral.

4 Agia Ekaterini
At the foot of the square, and more interesting than the cathedral, is this church which in the 16th century was one of the great schools of Cretan icon painting. Today it houses the world's best collection of Cretan icons. ⏰ *10am–3pm Mon–Fri • Adm*

5 Plateia Venizelou
Leave Plateia Ekaterinis by its northwest corner, and walk east to Plateia Nikoforou Foka, then left to Plateia Venizelou. The Morosini fountain

Venetian fountain

For more on Irakleio See pp12–15 & 80

Left **Agia Ekaterini** Right **Venetian Fortress**

stands in the middle of the square, with two stone lions standing sentinel.

San Marco and the Loggia
On the southeast side of the square, the former Venetian Cathedral of San Marco, dedicated to Venice's patron saint, became a mosque and is now an exhibition centre and conference hall. Leave the square by 25 Augoustou and walk past the Loggia. If this Venetian town hall looks suspiciously modern, blame restoration after earthquake and bomb damage.

Agios Titos
Turn right immediately after the Loggia to find Agios Titos (St Titus). Originally Byzantine, the church was rebuilt by the Venetians, turned into a mosque by the Turks and reclaimed by the Orthodox church in 1925. Inside, a reliquary contains the skull of St Titus. ◈ 9am–5pm daily • Free

Historical Museum
Returning to 25 Augoustou, turn left onto Theotokopoulou, then left onto Gazi, which leads to the Historical Museum of Crete. The basement contains some interesting Venetian stonework, Turkish and Byzantine remnants and the only El Greco painting left in Crete. ◈ 9am–4:30pm Mon–Fri, 9am–2pm Sat • Adm

Venetian Fortress
Built in 1523–40 to guard the harbour approaches, the massive Rocca al Mare, as it was known to the Venetians, served its purpose well. Piles of cannonballs in the inner chambers seem to await another assault. ◈ 28102 88484 • 8:30am–3pm Tue–Sun • Adm

Venetian Arsenal (Arsenali)
On your way back from the fortress, you will see a series of high stone vaults built into the wall behind the harbour. These were the Arsenali or shipyards where the great galleys were built that gave Venice its control of the sea.

Agios Titos

Flavour of the Walk
Crete's bustling capital has a wealth of relics of its Venetian past tucked away in nooks and corners among its more modern buildings. Start this walk as early as you can – Irakleio becomes uncomfortably hot by early afternoon. Allow three to four hours.

Around the Island – Central Crete

Following pages **Nida Plateau and Mt Idi**

83

Left **Chersonisos resort** Right **Agia Galini beach**

TOP10 Beaches

Malia
A long strip of bars, clubs, shops, hotels and apartments lines the main coast highway at Malia. The splendid sandy beach is crowded with sun loungers and umbrellas from early summer until September. ◈ Map M4

Chersonisos
A big, brash resort that may soon grow to merge with neighbouring Stalida and Malia. The beach is unarguably superb, and has an array of multinational bars and restaurants. ◈ Map L3

Matala
A series of sandy coves separated by rocky headlands, Matala first attracted sun-seeking hippy travellers in the 1960s and graduated to become a small holiday resort in the 1980s. ◈ Map G6

Agia Galini
On a crescent bay where a reed-lined river meets the sea, this is a classic fishing village turned beach resort. ◈ Map G5

Bali
A small, purpose-built resort set around three coves sheltered by cliffs. Avoid the crowds from June to September. ◈ Map H3

Dytikos (Lendas)
One of the longest beaches on the south central coast, Dytikos is popular with nudist sunbathers. ◈ Map J6

Kato Gouves (Gouvia)
With its long stretch of sand and shingle and growing number of package holiday hotels, this is one of the better beaches close to Irakleio. ◈ Map L3

Panormos
One of the less developed beaches on the central north coast, Panormos has a small sandy beach beside a miniature fishing harbour and a few places to eat and drink. ◈ Map G3

Kaloi Limenes
A relatively remote and peaceful series of small beaches and coves among dramatic cliffs. But the offshore oil tanker terminal rather mars the view. ◈ Map H6

Irakleio
If you have time to kill while in the capital, head for the municipal beach at Amnisos, which is open from 9am to 7pm for a small fee. ◈ Map K3

Matala

Left **Malia beach** Right **Palace of Malia**

Best of the Rest

1 Museum of Cretan Ethnology, Vori
One of the first museums to celebrate the lives of ordinary Cretans (see p38).

2 Palace of Malia
Only 3 km (2 miles) inland from the bustling resort of modern Malia, a ruined Minoan palace seems to grow from the rocky hillside (see pp34–5).

3 Mt Giouchtas
Looming to the south of Archanes, Mt Giouchtas is the mythical burial place of the god Zeus. The remains of a Minoan sanctuary are below the summit, and the area has been declared a conservation area, with the aim of protecting eagles, vultures and other raptors. ◈ Map K4

4 Minoan Villa Site, Tylissos
Tylissos was inhabited more than 4,000 years ago, but the most interesting discoveries are the remains of three large Minoan villas. ◈ 23108 31241 • Map J4 • 8:30am–3pm daily • Adm

5 Archanes Archaeological Museum
The small farming town of Archanes has a surprisingly good museum with finds from nearby sites, including clay Minoan coffins, fragments of pottery, and a sacrificial dagger that may have been used in human sacrifice. ◈ Map K4 • 8:30am–2:30pm daily (summer only) • Adm

6 Church of Agios Mikhail Arkhangelos, Asomatos
The Archangel Michael, leader of the heavenly host, is known in Greek as "O Taxiarchis" (the Brigadier) and is depicted in armour, sword in hand, along with other saints in the frescoes within the pretty 14th-century church at Asomatos. ◈ Map K4

7 Koudouma Monastery
The monks of Koudouma live in enviable isolation in a tiny monastery on a sandy beach fringed with palm trees. ◈ Map J6 • Dawn to dusk daily • Donations welcome

8 Minoan Villa Site, Vathypetrou
Vathypetrou was presumably the home of a Minoan landowner, and ancient wine-making equipment found on the site indicates that the surrounding vineyards are thousands of years old. ◈ Map K4 • 8:30am–1pm daily • Adm

9 Mt Kofinas
A mere hillock by Cretan standards, but still a challenging climb (starting from Kapetaniana village) with great views of Mt Idi (see p53) and the south coast.

10 Cretaquarium, Irakleio
Situated just a 10-minute drive from Irakleio airport, this aquarium is home to 2,500 individual sea-creatures from 200 Mediterranean species. ◈ Map K4 • Summer: 9am–9pm daily; Winter: 9am–7pm daily

Left **Taverna Street, Agia Galini** Right **New York bar, Chersonisos**

TOP 10 Bars and Cafés

1 Ciao, Irakleio
The big, breezy self-service café beside the Morosini Fountain offers cold drinks, snacks, pizza, pasta and cooked breakfasts. ✆ *Plateia Venizelou • Map K3*

2 The Four Lions, Irakleio
A rooftop café open from early morning until late at night. It offers a panoramic view of the older part of Irakleio as well as cold drinks, snacks, wines, spirits and cocktails. ✆ *Plateia Venizelou*

3 Ta Leontaria, Irakleio
Beneath the city walls, this old-fashioned patisserie serves Greek coffee, frappé, espresso and cappuccino, ices and cream-filled pastries. ✆ *Plateia Venizelou*

4 MoCafe, Irakleio
Handily located opposite the Irakleio Archeological Museum, MoCafe has a cool, arched interior with marble floor and an eclectic collection of modern art on the walls. It serves filled baguettes, juices, shakes, beers and coffee. ✆ *Odos Sapoutiel*

5 Paradiso, Agia Galini
Large music bar close to the harbour, which only gets going after dinner, then rocks into the small hours, with loud music and a young clientele. ✆ *Taverna Street • Map G5*

6 Kafeneio, Matala
Bright and cheerful café-bar, offering fresh fruit juice and yoghurt for breakfast and cold drinks throughout the day. An internet café is upstairs. ✆ *Village square • Map G6*

7 Ouzeri Elisabeth, Malia
A quieter, more traditional island in Malia's sea of neon-lit cocktail bars. Choose from ouzos and meze and Cretan wine from the barrel. ✆ *Church square, Old Malia • Map M4*

8 Kipouli, Malia
Virtually 24-hour drinking is the main selling point of this bar, attracting those who like to party all night and sleep on the beach all day. ✆ *Centre of Old Malia • 5:50am–2am the next day*

9 New York, Chersonisos
On the beach close to the entrance of the harbour, New York starts the day as a beach bar serving breakfasts, snacks and cold drinks, and after sunset metamorphoses into a noisy, lively music bar. ✆ *Map L3*

10 Hard Rock Cafe, Chersonisos
The international Hard Rock brand offers a familiar blend of cold beer, burgers and cocktails, attracting locals and visitors. ✆ *East end of Eleftheros Venizelou*

Paradiso, Agia Galini

For more restaurants, tavernas, bars, cafés and ouzeries **See pp68–73**

Price Categories

For a three-course meal for one with half a bottle of wine (or equivalent meal), taxes and extra charges.

€ under €12
€€ €12–€18
€€€ €18–€24
€€€€ €24–€32
€€€€€ over €32

Left **Loukoulos restaurant, Irakleio**

Restaurants

1 Loukoulos, Irakleio
Probably the best restaurant in Irakleio, serving Italian cuisine in up-market surroundings (white linen tablecloths and candles in the evening) in a room decorated with antique prints and paintings.
⊗ *Korai 5 • 2810 224435 • €€€€€*

2 Giovanni, Irakleio
Cretan and Greek dishes as well as Italian and international cuisine in elegant surroundings. The lobster with filet mignon à la Café de Paris is a house speciality. ⊗ *Korai 12 • 2810 346338 • €€€€*

3 I Erganos, Irakleio
Hearty Cretan cooking in a family-run place. Specials include sygouri (meat soup) and a selection of grilled meat dishes.
⊗ *Georgiadou 5 • 2810 285629 • €€*

4 Ta Grousouzadika, Irakleio
Old-fashioned grill restaurant in Irakleio's market area. The lamb and pork chops, steak, chicken and sausages are excellent.
⊗ *Theodosaki 17, Irakleio • No tel • €€*

5 O Kyriakos, Irakleio
In traditional taverna style, you will be beckoned into the kitchen of this old-fashioned restaurant with smoke-stained, wood-panelled walls to choose your meal from bubbling pots or glass cases filled with fish, chops and vegetables. ⊗ *Leoforos Dimokratias 53 • 2810 222464 • €€*

6 Minos, Irakleio
Lamb baked with yoghurt is the speciality of this unassuming, cheerful restaurant which is as popular with Irakleians as it is with visitors. ⊗ *Dedalou 10 • €€*

7 Thalassina, Irakleio
This seafood restaurant has a wide array of freshly caught fish and shellfish, including well-prepared squid, cuttlefish, mussels and less challenging offerings such as lobster, sea bass and grilled tuna. The wine list comes from all over Greece.
⊗ *Kalon Limenon 27 • 2810 251378 • €€€*

8 Erotokritos, Ammoudara
Opened in 2003, this taverna serves traditional Cretan appetizers and main courses. Its white wine from the barrel is particularly good. ⊗ *Papandreou 109 • 2810 252426 • 11am–midnight all year • €€*

9 Old House Tavern, Malia
The international dishes and Greek favourites are good value at this restaurant in the old part of Malia, which has tables in a shady courtyard. ⊗ *Arkadiou 25 • Closed Nov–Mar • €€*

10 Electra Restaurant, Stalida
A multinational restaurant including Italian, Chinese and Indian thali dishes as well as many Greek favourites. ⊗ *Main street • 28970 31938 • Closed Nov–Mar • €€€*

Left **Firkas Fort, Chania** Centre **Market stall, Rethymno** Right **The beach at Rethymno**

Western Crete

WESTERN CRETE IS IN MANY WAYS *the most exciting part of the island. Much of the west is dominated by the jagged, treeless peaks of the Lefka Ori (White Mountains), which may be capped by snow until June. Traversed by spectacular gorges, the mountains drop sharply to the Libyan Sea on Crete's south coast. These mountains were for centuries the heartland of Cretan resistance to foreign occupiers of the island. Many of the remoter villages were accessible only on foot until the second half of the 20th century, and a traditional way of life lingered longer here than in other parts of the island. The west also has Crete's two most attractive towns, Chania and Rethymno, and some of the best beaches, ranging from pebbly coves to long swathes of golden sand.*

🔟 Sights in Western Crete

1. Rethymno
2. Chania
3. Samaria Gorge
4. Paleochora
5. Frangokastello
6. Sougia
7. Loutro
8. Georgioupoli
9. Plakias
10. Kastelli Kissamou

Villager, Sougia

Chania harbour

1 Rethymno
Rethymno is Crete's third largest town (after Irakleio and Chania) and its most attractive, with an inner harbour overlooked by a huge, brooding Venetian fortress (the Fortetsa), streets of old-fashioned Venetian mansions, and a palm-fringed esplanade along a sandy beach. Thanks to its nearby beaches, Rethymno has become a fully fledged resort town, with holiday hotels east of the city centre, and lots of shops, restaurants, bars and cafés. It also has a colourful early morning market on Thursday and Saturday (see pp22–3 & 94–5).

Nerandzes Mosque, Rethymno

2 Chania
Chania, Crete's second largest city, is built around a fine natural harbour which attracted a host of settlers over the millennia, from early Minoans to Romans, Byzantines, Saracens, Venetians and Turks. The heart of the city is the old town, a huddle of narrow streets sheltered by a ring of battlements built by the Venetians; under their rule Chania was one of Crete's most important ports. Today the old town is dominated by restaurants, cafés and bars, while outside the Venetian walls is the newer part of town. Chania has some of Crete's most spectacular scenery as backdrop, with the slopes of the Lefka Ori range (White Mountains) rising steeply a short way inland and seeming to dominate the entire southern horizon (see pp18–19).

3 Samaria Gorge
Taking its name from the tiny Venetian church of Santa Maria (close to the now abandoned Samaria village), this is probably the most dramatic stretch of scenery in Crete. The gorge is one of the deepest and longest in Europe, cutting its way through the Lefka Ori from the Omalos Plateau to the Libyan Sea, and narrowing to a width of only a few arm widths at its narrowest point. The gorge is within the Samaria National Park, a refuge for many rare birds, plants and mammals (see pp26–7).

Samaria Gorge

Paleochora

Paleochora

Paleochora stands on a peninsula between two beaches: a long sandy bay to the northwest and an even longer, but pebblier and more exposed beach, to the southeast. Close to the centre of the village are the ruined walls of a Venetian fort, Castel Selino, which was built to guard the harbour and coast but left to crumble after the Turkish conquest. "Discovered" by backpackers in the 1970s, Paleochora is now one of Crete's quieter resorts, with a low-key nightlife and a family atmosphere. Map B4

Frangokastello

A small, deserted "Castle of the Franks" – actually built in 1371 by the Venetians to defend this stretch of the south coast against pirate attacks *(see p40)* – gives this small fishing village and resort its name. The Lion of St Mark, symbol of the Venetian Republic, still adorns the town's southern gateway. Frangokastello has a long sweep of grey sandy beach, and offers, by way of accommodation, small pensions and apartments. A handful of restaurants and cafés open up in summer, but the choice of places to eat, drink and stay is very limited in the low season. Map E4

Bandit Country

The Sfakia region lived by its own fierce laws for generations, and vendettas between local families were not uncommon even a couple of generations back. Prosperity and communications have tamed the region somewhat, but many Sfakiots still have an illicit firearm or two (often of World War II vintage) hidden away in the attic – and in the remoter parts it seems that no road sign has escaped target practice.

Sougia

Sougia is perfect for anyone in search of peace, quiet and isolation. Tourism is very low-key, with just a scattering of small pensions and guest houses, tavernas and cafés. The town's beach is long and pebbly, and the water is sparklingly clear, while an hour's walk away are the ruins of the ancient city-state of Lissos, including a temple to Asklepios, the god of healing, which dates from the 3rd century BC. Map C4

Sougia beach

Left **Loutro** Right **Georgioupoli**

7 Loutro

Sheltered by a stretch of headland and dwarfed by the near-vertical slopes of the Lefka Ori (White Mountains) above it, Loutro is one of the most charming spots on Crete. Less than 30 years ago Loutro had only a few elderly inhabitants and one taverna. Tourism has changed all that, and now dazzling white pensions and apartments sit above the tiny crescent-shaped beach. Accessible only on foot (by a precarious cliff path) or by boat from Chora Sfakion, Loutro seems unlikely to be over-run by tourism, and is ideal for a laid-back holiday. ✪ Map D4

8 Georgioupoli

A modern community by Cretan standards, the town was founded little over a century ago when it was named in honour of Prince George, the then governor of Crete. More recently, it has become a resort, with hotels stretching along the sandy beach. It attracts a less raucous clientele than resorts such as Malia and Chersonisos, however, and the heart of Georgioupoli is a town square, shaded by eucalyptus and plane trees. ✪ Map E3

9 Plakias

Plakias is one of Crete's newer resorts. Its excellent beaches were overlooked by the holiday industry until the 1990s, at which point, the tiny fishing and farming community began to transform into a strip of purpose-built hotels (none of them obtrusively large), apartments, shops and restaurants. Not for those looking for authenticity, Plakias nevertheless has plenty going for it, including attractive surrounding countryside, its own long sweep of shingly sand, and lots more even prettier beaches and palm-fringed coves within walking distance. ✪ Map F4

10 Kastelli Kissamou

Usually known simply as Kastelli, Crete's westernmost town is couched in a bay between the Rodopou and Gramvoussa peninsulas. It has largely missed out on the tourism boom, although it has a handful of hotels and restaurants. There are several rarely-visited ancient and medieval sites nearby, including the ruins of Polyrinia (see p41), and there are reasonable – if unexceptional by Cretan standards – beaches on either side of town. ✪ Map B2

Plakias

Left **Market** Right **Folk Art Museum**

🔟 A Morning in Rethymno

1 Porta Guora

Make an early start at Plateia Tessaron Martyron, the large square from which the Venetian Porta Guora – the only intact remnant of the Venetian city walls – leads into the old town. The Tessaron Martyron (Four Martyrs) Church at the northeast corner of the square honours four Cretans executed in 1824 by the Turks for remaining secretly Christian despite an apparent conversion to Islam. A pointed minaret by the church is all that is left of one of the city's Turkish mosques.

2 The Market

Passing through the gate, walk north on Ethnikis Antistasis, which bustles with produce stalls, small open-fronted shops and cafés serving tiny glasses of raki and cups of coffee. This is a great place to buy Cretan herbs, honey or olive oil to take home.

3 Agios Frangiskos

Follow Ethnikis Antistasis north to the Church of Agios Frangiskos (St Francis), which was formerly part of a Venetian Roman Catholic monastery. The doorway is beautifully carved and the basilica is still used by the town's small Roman Catholic community.

Nerantzes Mosque

4 Nerantzes Mosque

At the north end of Ethnikis Antistasis is the Nerantzes Mosque, the town's best preserved Ottoman relic dating back to the 17th century. It is now a music school and concert hall, and its slender, pointed minaret can be seen from some distance. It was previously a Catholic church dedicated to Santa Maria. Although the building has been fully restored, the original doorway remains.

5 Historical and Folk Art Museum

Back at street level, turn left onto Vernardou and, midway along on your left, step into the Historical and Folk Art Museum, with its collection of tools, textiles and traditional costume (see also p23). 🖉 28 Vernardou
• 9:30am–2pm Mon–Sat
• Adm

Market flower stall

For more on Rethymno, see pp22–23 & 91

Rethymno harbour

Venetian Loggia

This elegant 16th-century loggia is a poignant reminder of Venice's reign and has survived almost intact. The visible walls have equal semi-circular arches, with the middle one serving as the entrance to the ground floor. It is now a museum and art gallery *(see also p23)*. ◎ *Palaiológou & Arkadíou • Mar–Sep daily • Adm*

Rimondi Fountain

Turn right again on Arabatzoglou, which leads down to Petihaki, a small square crammed with cafés. Stop for a drink and snack at Zanafoti, an old-fashioned café close to the 17th-century Rimondi Fountain, built in 1627 to supply part of the old town with fresh drinking water.

Rethymno Archaeological Museum

From the square, bear left past the fountain, along Mesolongiou and Himaras, to the Rethymno Archaeological Museum, which displays Minoan coffins and burial goods, as well as Neolithic and Roman finds *(see also p36)*. ◎ *Cheimarras • 8:30am–3pm Tue–Sun • Adm*

The Fortetza

From the museum, cross Katehaki to the Fortetza, built in 1573 by the Venetians *(see also pp22 & 40)*. This massive fortress was built in response to the threat of Turkish invasion, but in the end it proved no match for the might of the Ottoman Empire. ◎ *Katechaki • 10am–5pm daily • Adm*

Venetian Harbour

Conclude your tour down at the pretty Venetian (or Inner) Harbour, and treat yourself to a seafood lunch at Mourayio Maria, set in a 16th-century building with quayside tables. ◎ *Nearchou 45 • 28310 26475 • Apr–Oct daily*

Fortetza

Flavour of the Walk

Built by the Venetians, Rethymno's old quarter preserves a pleasantly old-fashioned air, with narrow streets and lanes lined with tall old stucco-fronted town houses. Venetian and Turkish drinking fountains are tucked away down side streets, and the domes and spires of the city's surviving mosques – now used for secular purposes – are reminders of its multi-cultural history. This walk around the old quarter takes no more than three hours.

Left **Falasarna** Right **Stavros**

🔟 Beaches

Around the Island – Western Crete

Preveli (Finikas)
The Kourtaliotis river meets the sea at Preveli, where the green river, blue sea, date palms and "Greek bamboo" (calamus reeds) create a tropical oasis feel. ◈ Map F5

Falasarna
This long sweep of yellow sand is one of the finest on the west coast, and has yet to be exploited by the tourist industry – though there are a few places to stay. ◈ Map A2

Platanias
The best beach within easy reach of Chania, and the village has plenty of places to eat and drink. This is Chania's after-dark summer playground, with pubs, clubs and discos. ◈ Map C2

Stavros
Quieter than Platanias, and so an attractive alternative for those seeking a little tranquillity. The lagoon-like bay featured in the film *Zorba the Greek*. ◈ Map D2

Agios Pavlos
At the foot of the Samaria Gorge, and so perfect for a

Platanias

restorative swim in its cool waters after the downhill hike. ◈ Map D4

Elafonisi
The superb beach opposite the island of Elafonisi on the west coast is one of Crete's best, with a long crescent of white sand and shallow turquoise water that warms up quickly in summer. Very busy. ◈ Map A4

Sougia
Shaded in places by a line of Tamarisk trees, Sougia's position between Paleochora and Agia Roumeli makes it ideal for a quick plunge for walkers treading a coastal route. ◈ Map C4

Marmara (Marble Beach)
A collection of sheltered coves lined with smooth white pebbles. Marmara attracts nude sunbathers and can be reached by boat from Loutro. ◈ Map D4

Glika Nera (Sweetwater Beach)
A tiny patch of pebble and sand reachable only by scrambling along a rocky cliff path, or by boat from Loutro or Chora Sfakion. Often used by nudists. ◈ Map D4

Damnoni
Its golden sands have been somewhat marred by insensitive hotel building, but east of the main beach are smaller sandy coves, Ammoudi and Skinaria. ◈ Map F4

Previous pages **Frangokastello**

Left **Chora Sfakion** Right **Archaia Eleftherna**

Best of the Rest

Moni Gonia, Rodopou Peninsula

Anogeia
1 Pleasant cafés and shops conceal Anogeia's embattled past, when it was a hotbed of resistance against the Turks, who sacked it in 1821 and 1826, and the Germans, who levelled it in 1944. ◈ *Map H4*

Chora Sfakion
2 A major rendezvous point for excursion groups who arrive by boat having walked the Samaria Gorge. Once they have found their coaches, the town returns to its pleasant slumber. ◈ *Map D4*

Archaia Eleftherna
3 Founded in 700 BC, ancient Eleftherna was a powerful Dorian city. Having vanished from history, it is now being rediscovered by archaeologists. ◈ *Map G3 • 8.30am–7pm daily • Free*

Polyrinia
4 Wonderful views surround the broken walls and foundations of this ancient Acropolis, upon which stands an equally ruined Venetian fortress *(see p41)*.

Monastery of Agia Irini
5 This restored 14th-century monastery is now a nunnery and also a centre for traditional weaving and needlework.
◈ *Map F3 • 8am–2pm and 5–8pm*

Aptera
6 A Byzantine town built on the site of a Hellenistic city, remains here include Roman cisterns, Byzantine foundations, a Venetian monastery and a Turkish fort.
◈ *Map D2 • 8.30am–7pm • Free*

Gramvoussa Peninsula
7 The remote and barely populated Gramvoussa Peninsula has one of Crete's best beaches at Falasarna, where there are also the scattered remains of a Hellenistic city. ◈ *Map B1–2*

Rodopou Peninsula
8 A barren peninsula that attracted the Orthodox monks who built the monastery of Moni Gonia, which has several fine icons. ◈ *Moni Gonia • Map B1–2 • 8am–2pm and 5–8pm*

Akrotiri Peninsula
9 Monks have been drawn to Crete's peninsulas – Akrotiri's best monasteries are the abandoned Moni Katholikou and the Venetian Moni Gouverneto *(see p42)*.

War Cemetery
10 The burial place of more than 1,500 Allied soldiers who died during the Battle of Crete, in May 1941. ◈ *Map D2*

Left **Synagogi Bar, Chania** Centre **Kafeneion O Minares, Rethymno** Right **La Jetee, Paleochora**

TOP10 Bars and Cafés

1 Ta Dio Lux, Chania
The best place in town for a sundown cocktail. Tables with a view are at a premium, though, as this is currently Chania's trendiest bar. ✆ *Sarpidona*

2 Synagogi Bar, Chania
This popular bar is set in the large courtyard of a Venetian ruin that was once a synagogue. Cosy corner sofas and quiet music provide a low-key atmosphere. ✆ *12 Skoufon St, Old Harbour*

3 Point Bar, Chania
A small but lively bar. For a quieter drink take a table on the outdoor balcony and watch the world go by in the square below. ✆ *Plateia Syntrivani, Old Harbour*

4 Epohes (Four Seasons Bar), Chania
Dance the night away at this fashionable bar on the west harbour. Alternatively, you can cool down with a refreshing drink at one of the outdoor harbour front tables. ✆ *Akti Koundourioti, Old Harbour*

5 Raki Bar Pandelis, Sougia
Old-fashioned wooden chairs, marble-topped tables and a vine-covered verandah are part of the appeal. Its interior – a vaulted bar with a wooden floor, set in an old stone building – is attractive too. ✆ *Sougia*

6 Kafeneion O Minares, Rethymno
A rare authentic taverna, serving thimbles of Greek coffee and glasses of *tsikondia* (a strong spirit) to a clientele of venerable locals. ✆ *Plateia Petihaki*

7 Utopia Bar, Platanias
West Crete's main summer night scene revolves around the resort of Platanias. Utopia is a lively, friendly bar playing the latest sounds as well as old favourites. ✆ *Main Street*

8 Kafeneion Yannis, Paleochora
A simple, old-fashioned ouzeri on the town's main street. Do not expect a list of sophisticated cocktails; do expect an authentic Cretan atmosphere. ✆ *Odos Venizelos*

9 La Jetee, Paleochora
Attracting more holidaymakers than locals, Jetee's fancy drinks carry equally fancy prices. Overlooking the sandy beach on the west side of Paleochora, it is at its liveliest in the evening. ✆ *Sandy Beach*

10 Nostos Disco Bar, Paleochora
Best of the music bars along Pebble Beach. Rock, pop and dance music is occasionally interspersed with Cretan dancing to traditional lyra rhythms. ✆ *Pebble Beach*

Kafeneion Yannis, Paleochora

For more restaurants, tavernas, bars, cafés and ouzeries
See pp68–73

Price Categories

For a three-course meal for one with half a bottle of wine (or equivalent meal), taxes and extra charges.

€	under €12
€€	12–€18
€€€	€18–€24
€€€€	€24–€32
€€€€€	over €32

Left **Veneto**, Rethymno Right **Kyria Maria**, Rethymno

🔟 Restaurants

1 Ela, Chania
Within the courtyard of an old Venetian mansion, Ela serves a wide menu, including standard Greek dishes and a few authentically Cretan offerings. 🔾 *42 Kondylaki • 28210 74128 • Closed Nov–Mar • €€€*

Ela, Chania

2 Kariatis, Chania
This renowned Italian restaurant serves a wide variety of tasty dishes and is set in beautiful surroundings among Venetian ruins. 🔾 *12 Katehaki Sq, Old Harbour • 28210 55600 • €€€€€*

3 Tamam, Chania
A wide range of Greek, Levantine and Cretan dishes, with a better choice of non-meat dishes than most of its rivals. 🔾 *49 Zambeliou • 28210 96080 • €€€€*

4 Karnagio, Chania
Karnagio serves substantial taverna meals, the traditional favourites including grilled meats and huge peasant salads with feta cheese. 🔾 *8 Katehaki • 28210 53366 • Closed Nov–Mar • €€€*

5 Veneto, Rethymno
Set in 13th-century vaults beneath the Veneto Hotel, the restaurant serves Cretan specialities within a beautiful setting, with stone-flagged floors, mosaics and antique furniture. 🔾 *4 Epimenidou • 28310 56634 • €€€€€*

6 Avli, Rethymno
With its pretty garden setting, this is one of the town's finest. Mainly grilled and roasted meats, and Cretan favourites such as *apatzia* sausages and roasted goat. 🔾 *22 Xanthoudidou • 28310 26213 • €€€€*

7 Kyria Maria, Rethymno
This little taverna in the old quarter serves plain, village-style dishes. It fairly bustles in the evenings but is quieter at lunch time. Great value. 🔾 *20 Moschovitou • 28310 29078 • Closed Nov–Mar • €€€*

8 Taverna tou Zissi, Rethymno
On the old Irakleio highway, 4km (2 miles) east of Rethymno, Zissi's charcoal-grilled lamb and chicken are worth the short trip from town. 🔾 *Missiria • 28310 28814 • €€€*

9 Oriental Bay, Paleochora
This quiet restaurant serves Cretan and other Greek dishes and is very popular with locals. Pleasant courtyard. 🔾 *East Beach • 28230 41322 • Closed mid-Oct–May • €*

10 Sterna tou Bloumosifi, Vamos
Part of a restored 19th-century stone village, Sterna tou Bloumosifi serves Cretan specialities baked in wood-burning ovens. 🔾 *28250 22932 • €€€*

Left **Ancient bath, Archaeological Museum, Agios Nikolaos** Centre **Siteia** Right **Market, Siteia**

Eastern Crete

CRETE'S FAR EAST *is a little less rugged than the wild west, and less populous than the central region of the island. It also sees rather fewer package holidaymakers, mainly because of its remoteness from the island's airports. That said, the region's largest town, Agios Nikolaos, is a thriving holiday resort, while Crete's most expensive and exclusive hotel and villa complexes can be found around Elounda, on the Gulf of Mirabello. The east also has good beaches, on its north, south and east coasts, notably the famous palm beach at Vai, and there are Minoan ruins to be seen at Gournia, Mochlos, Zakros and elsewhere.*

TOP 10 Sights in Eastern Crete

1. Agios Nikolaos
2. Siteia
3. Vai
4. Zakros Gorge
5. Elounda
6. Makrygialos
7. Spinalonga
8. Ierapetra
9. Lato
10. Mochlos

Agios Nikolaos

Agios Nikolaos harbour

Agios Nikolaos

Agios Nikolaos has the most attractive location of any town in eastern Crete. By the Gulf of Mirabello, it is built around an inner lagoon, Voulismeni, which is surrounded by palm trees and cafés. Modern hotels and apartments dwarf the surviving older buildings, but it is still a place of considerable charm. There is a small town beach, and boats take holidaymakers to larger beaches nearby. The town takes its name from the tiny 11th-century church of Agios Nikolaos (which now stands in the grounds of the Minos Palace Hotel. The Archaeological Museum *(see p37)* displays numerous finds from nearby sites including Mochlos and Gournia. ◈ *Map N4*

Siteia

Siteia looks surprisingly modern but was founded in the 4th century, when a flourishing Byzantine city stood here. Its fortunes waned after the 14th century, when it was damaged by earthquakes and sacked by corsairs. It was not until the late 19th century that Siteia became an important farming centre, surrounded by olive groves and vineyards. It has a picturesque harbour overlooked by a Venetian fortress and an Archaeological Museum *(see p36)*. Siteia is becoming an important area for the production of quality Cretan wines. ◈ *Map Q4*

Vai

The main claim to fame of the beach at Vai is in having the only wild palm grove in Europe. The palm forest apparently existed at least 2,000 years ago, so may have been planted by early navigators from the Middle East who came to Crete. The drawbacks are that the palm trees are fenced off and protected, and the beach becomes overrun with visitors in high season. Nevertheless, it is beautiful, especially if visited outside the busiest summer months of June, July and August. ◈ *Map R4*

Vai

Left **Zakros Gorge** Right **Taverna, Kato Zakros**

4 Zakros Gorge

The Zakros Gorge is known locally as the Valley of the Dead because the numerous caves in its limestone walls were used as tombs in Roman times. The gorge runs from the peaceful village of Ano ("upper") Zakros to Kato ("lower") Zakros on the sea, near an ancient Minoan palace site rediscovered in 1961. It is a beautiful and not too challenging 8-km (5-mile) hike *(see also p53)*. ◈ *Map Q5*

5 Elounda

Elounda, on the Gulf of Mirabello, is Crete's most expensive resort area, with several exclusive villa and hotel complexes in landscaped grounds. Several of these even have private beaches. The village itself is less up-market, with a clutter of shops and restaurants surrounding a small fishing harbour from which boats depart daily in summer on

Elounda harbour

The Caves of Crete

About 5,000 caverns and potholes riddle the island's mountain slopes. Grottoes have yielded fascinating relics of the ancient world, indicating that Crete was inhabited for thousands of years before the rise of the Minoan civilization. Only a handful have been fully charted, and thousands more remain to be fully explored and mapped.

---

trips to Spinalonga, the Venetian fortress-island and former leper colony not far offshore. ◈ *Map N4*

6 Makrygialos

Makrygialos is the most popular holiday resort on the southeast coast, with a long, straggling array of small pensions, hotels and tavernas stretching along a crescent of rather wind-swept, gently shelving sand and pebble beach, which is the best in this part of the island. ◈ *Map P5*

7 Spinalonga

The fortifications covering this small, rocky island in the Gulf of Mirabello were built by the Venetians in 1579 to control the approaches to this superb natural

For the archaeological site of Gournia **see pp30–31**

harbour. Superior sea power allowed Venice to hang onto Spinalonga for half a century after the fall of the rest of Crete to the Turks, and it was surrendered only in 1715. Used as a leper colony in the first half of the 20th century, its buildings are now very dilapidated, but the grim walls may still give the visitor an eerie thrill. 🔍 *Map N4*

Ruins on Spinalonga

Ierapetra
Ierapetra is the largest town on the southeast coast. Its buildings are rather dull, but it has a good, long beach of grey sand and the distinction of receiving more hours of sunshine per year than anywhere else in Europe. Huge crops of tomatoes are raised all year round in the surrounding farmlands. Ierapetra became an important Dorian Greek settlement as early as the 8th century BC, and by the 2nd century BC it was the largest city-state on the island after defeating its Eteocretan neighbours, Praisos and Itanos. Under the Romans it was an important seaport; the Venetians built a fortress to defend the harbour. 🔍 *Map N6*

Myrtos beach, near Ierapetra

Lato
Modern-day Agios Nikolaos was once no more than the seaport annex of this Dorian Greek city which flourished between the 7th and 3rd centuries BC. Built around two neighbouring hills, 8 km (5 miles) west of Agios Nikolaos, Lato is the best preserved Dorian site in Crete, with walls built of massive stone blocks. There are fine views over the Gulf of Mirabello from its *agora* (market-place) in a saddle between the twin summits. 🔍 *Map M4*
• *8:30am–3pm Tue–Sun* • *Adm*

Mochlos
Mochlos, 32 km (20 miles) east of Agios Nikolaos on the coast road, is a tiny fishing hamlet with a handful of tavernas. Just offshore is the island of Mochlos, which in ancient times was connected to the mainland by an isthmus. This has been eroded by earthquakes and waves. On the island are the remains of Minoan houses and a Minoan harbour, much of which is now under water. Seal stones, superb gold jewellery and vases carved from quartz, alabaster and black steatite have been discovered in rock tombs on the island and are displayed in the Agios Nikolaos and Siteia archaeological museums. 🔍 *Map P4*

Left **Ancient steps, Gournia** Centre **Boat near Vai** Right **Heron, Zakros**

TOP 10 A Day's Drive in Eastern Crete

1 Gournia

Early in the morning, on any day except a Monday, head east out of Agios Nikolaos on the main coast highway. Gournia is south of the road, 24 km (15 miles) east of Agios Nikolaos. Try to arrive when it opens at 8:30am and allow a couple of hours to explore this well preserved Minoan site *(see pp30–31).* ✆ *Map N5*

2 Mochlos

Leaving Gournia, drive on along the coast highway to Mochlos, 11 km (7 miles) east of Gournia. This tiny fishing hamlet has a handful of tavernas, and a small boat will take you to the pretty island where the foundations of Minoan houses are seen. ✆ *Map P4*

3 Siteia

Siteia, once a Byzantine city, was destroyed in the 14th century, then rebuilt by a far-sighted local *pasha* (Ottoman governor) in the late 19th century *(see p103).* It has a picturesque harbour overlooked by a Venetian fortress and and an Archaeological Museum with Minoan treasures. Stop here for coffee, a cold drink or a snack at Zorbas, an old-fashioned café and taverna on the harbour. ✆ *Map Q4*

4 Moni Toplou

A 10-km (6-mile) drive from Siteia takes you along the north coast to Moni Toplou, a spectacular fortified monastery, founded in the 14th century, with sturdy stone walls around an inner courtyard with three tiers of tiny monks' cells. Within its small church, are some remarkable icons, including one of the finest in Crete, *Lord Thou Art Great,* by Ioannis Kornaros *(see also P57).* ✆ *Map Q4*

5 Vai

A further 6 km (4 miles) brings you to Vai *(see p103),* the easternmost point of this drive, on a peninsula which stretches towards Crete's northeast tip (inaccessible as it is a military area). Vai's famous palm forest is now a conservation area. The

Harbour life, Siteia

Left **Via beach** Right **Ierapetra harbour**

beach is very crowded in high season, but for a little more seclusion you can walk for 20–30 minutes to the less crowded coves at Itanos. ◈ *Map R4*

6 Zakros

After visiting Vai, turn south, through the small villages of Palaiokastro, Azokeramos, Adravasti and Ano Zakros, where you turn east for 8 km (5 miles) down a narrow road to reach Kato Zakros, on the sea. Stop here for a fish lunch at the Zakros Taverna. If you have the time and inclination, explore the Minoan palace *(see p35)*. ◈ *Map Q5*

7 Praisos

From Kato Zakros, retrace your tracks as far as Ano Zakros, then drive for 18 km (11 miles) through the villages of Ziros and Chandras to the ancient site at Praisos *(see p35)*. ◈ *Map Q5*

8 Lithines

Rejoin the main road and drive south for 8 km (5 miles) to the village of Lithines, built by tenants of the aristocratic Lithinos family in about the 10th century AD. Now a ghost village, it has two fine 15th-century churches. ◈ *Map Q5*

9 Makrygialos

The south coast of Crete is now only 10 km (6 miles) away.

Stop for a late afternoon swim at Makrygialos, a popular beach resort with the best beach in this part of the island. Either stay here for your evening meal or continue to Ierapetra. ◈ *Map P5*

10 Ierapetra

It is a 45-minute drive to Ierapetra, the largest town on the southeast coast, passing rank on rank of greenhouses, which produce bumper crops of tomatoes, peppers and cucumbers. Ierapetra – originally named Ierapytna – was Crete's most important Dorian Greek city in the 2nd century BC *(see p105)*. Unlike most Cretan towns, Ierapetra is still more interested in farming than in the package holiday business and is a good place to glimpse everyday life on Crete. From here, it's a 32-km (20-mile) evening drive back to Agios Nikolaos. ◈ *Map N6*

Flavour of the Tour

This round trip from Agios Nikolaos covers around 200 km (125 miles). Allow one full day to give yourself time to explore the archaeological site at Gournia and to stop off at some of the other places mentioned. Roads are mostly well surfaced, and traffic is light. All sights and stops along the way are well signposted (in Greek and English).

Left **Siteia** Centre **Xerocampos** Right **Mirtos**

Beaches

1 Vai
Vai's beach is certainly the most scenic in eastern Crete, with yellow sand and a grove of date palms giving it a truly tropical appearance. ✆ Map R4

2 Siteia
Unlike most larger Cretan coastal towns, Siteia has a perfectly good beach right on its doorstep that is great for windsurfing. ✆ Map Q4

3 Xerokampos
A tiny village with a series of small, sandy east-facing coves, one of the few coast places not yet discovered by the package tourism industry. ✆ Map Q5

4 Kato Zakros
At the foot of the Zakros Gorge, Kato Zakros has a crescent of sand and pebble beach, with a small fishing harbour and a handful of pensions and tavernas. ✆ Map R5

5 Makrygialos
The best beach on the southeast coast. A long strip of

Beachside taverna, Kato Zakros

sand interspersed with pebbles shelves gently into deeper water. ✆ Map P5

6 Mirtos
An amiably unpretentious farming and fishing village with a long, south-facing shingle beach, which is far less crowded than most in eastern Crete, even in high summer. ✆ Map M6

7 Kouremenos
Kouremenos is less than ideal for sunbathing because of strong breezes for most of the year. Those same breezes, however, make it a favourite windsurfing spot, with best conditions in summer usually in the afternoon. ✆ Map R4

8 Chionia
Rates a European Blue Flag for clean sand and water. There are even better, more secluded beaches to the south. ✆ Map R4

9 Milatos
A pebbly beach and surprisingly uncrowded compared with the teeming resorts only a few kilometres to the west. ✆ Map M4

10 Istro
Looks spectacular from a distance, with a sandy beach hemmed in by cliffs. But it is often heavily littered with flotsam and jetsam. ✆ Map N5

Around the Island – Eastern Crete

Left **Handwoven rugs, Kritsa** Centre **Lithines** Right **Moni Kapsa**

Other Attractions

1 Praisos
Based on clay statuettes and inscriptions found here, archaeologists believe it was a post-Minoan Eteocretan city *(see p35)*.

2 Moni Toplou
Fortified monastery founded in the 14th century. Its massive walls were built to protect it from pirates *(see p42)*.

3 Pelekita Cave, Kato Zakros
Just 2 km (1.5 miles) northeast of Kato Zakros village and a few hundred metres north of the Zakros Gorge *(see p104)*, the Pelekita cavern is one of the longest in Crete. ◈ *Map R5*

4 Kritsa
Overlooked by Mt Kastelleos, Kritsa stands at the edge of a wide and fertile plain and is regarded as one of Crete's most important craft centres. ◈ *Map M5*

5 Itanos
Just north of Vai, Itanos has three small pebble and shingle beaches that are never as crowded as Vai's stretch of golden sand. The scant remains of an ancient city can be seen on the low hills beyond. ◈ *Map R4*

6 Rousa Eklisia
Pretty village worth visiting for its superb view of the bay. Large plane trees shade the village square, and a stream feeds a natural fountain next to an old church. ◈ *Map Q5*

7 Lithines
Named for its founders, the Litinos clan of Byzantine nobles, the village has two 15th-century churches, Agios Athanasios and Tis Panagias. ◈ *Map Q5*

8 Moni Kapsa
A monastery that seems to merge into the cliffs, with the mummified body of a monk in its chapel. ◈ *Map Q6* • 8:30am–noon, 4–7pm

9 Pefki Gorge
A four-hour walk from Pefki to Makrygialos will take you along a dry river bed of white pebbles that runs through a canyon of weird rock formations. ◈ *Map P5*

Itanos

10 Voila
Deserted medieval village in rolling hill country, with a dilapidated Venetian tower standing guard over roofless cottages. The small church of Agios Georgios is well preserved. ◈ *Map Q5*

Café du Lac, Agios Nikolaos

TOP 10 Bars and Cafés

1 Café du Lac, Agios Nikolaos

Ices, cocktails, soft drinks, freshly squeezed orange juice and milk shakes. Also has an internet café area where you can pick up your e-mail. ✆ 28 Oktobriou 17

2 Café Zygos, Agios Nikolaos

Bar with a lake view and garden terrace shaded by greenery – a romantic place to laze away an afternoon or enjoy a pre-dinner cocktail or after-dinner digestif. ✆ Palaeologou

3 Anna Bei 1900, Ierapetra

In an old house which has been imaginatively refurbished to create bars, a café and a restaurant, this is the most attractive place for a drink in Ierapetra. ✆ N. Fonadiakis 8

4 Odeion, Ierapetra

On a summer evening, the garden of this graceful Neo-Classical building is an especially pleasant place to quaff a drink and absorb the last of the day's sun. ✆ Lasthenou, off Plateia Venizelou

5 Creperie Mike, Siteia

Owned by an expatriate Belgian, Mike's offers sweet and savoury crepes on a breezy terrace by the sea. ✆ Venizelou 162

6 Armida Boat Club, Agios Nikolaos

This café-bar, on a 1920s freighter in the outer harbour, makes a wonderfully serene spot for after dinner drinks. ✆ West Quay

7 Hellas, Elounda

One of the livelier spots in town, with live Cretan music and Greek pop most weekends. ✆ Elounda village; closed Nov–May

8 Veterano, Ierapetra

A newly fashionable terrace café ideal for a leisurely breakfast and just as good for a sundowner. ✆ Plateia Eleftherias

9 Ouzeri Manos, Ierapetra

A good spot for leisurely ouzo sipping and meze snacking, amid a string of tavernas, bars and cafés that stretch between the Venetian Fortress and the ferry pier. ✆ Samouil

10 Amnesia, Kato Zakros

The place to go after dark if you are looking for more than a quiet brandy, if only for the fact that this is the resort's sole gesture towards an upbeat nightlife. ✆ Seafront

Café Zygos, Agios Nikolaos

For more restaurants, tavernas, bars, cafés and ouzeries
See pp68–73

Left **Zorbas, Siteia** Right **Fish from Zakros**

🔟 Places to Eat

1 The Old Mill, Elounda
The most luxurious restaurant in eastern Crete, situated in the Elounda Mare Hotel (see p126). The menu combines the best of Greece with international cuisine. Booking essential; dress code formal. 🔌 Elounda Mare Hotel • 28410 41102 • Closed Nov–Mar • €€€€€

2 Kalidon, Elounda
Dining aboard a floating pontoon moored in Elounda's small fishing harbour, with a mix of Greek and international dishes. 🔌 Elounda Harbour • 28410 41451 • Closed Nov–Mar • €

3 Zorbas, Siteia
A long-established taverna serving freshly grilled fish and lobster, traditional Cretan dishes, charcoal-grilled meats and meze. 🔌 Harbourfront • 28430 22689 • €€

4 Tavern Kato Zakros Bay, Kato Zakros
On a terrace overlooking the sea, this restaurant serves fish, game and vegetarian meals. 🔌 Beachfront • 28430 26887 • Closed Nov–Apr • €€

5 Kalliontzis, Koutsouras
This friendly taverna offers home-cooked meals, set at outside tables overhung by tamarisk trees. 🔌 Seafront • 28430 51207 • Closed Nov–Apr • €€

6 Taverna Pelagos, Agios Nikolaos
A fine old taverna close to the fishing harbour, noted locally for its seafood. Its courtyard suits summer dining. 🔌 Korakaiand Katehaki • 28410 25737 • Closed Nov–Mar • €€

7 Poulis, Elounda Village
Catering mainly for visitors, the menu encompasses Greek and international dishes, a long list of grilled seafood and a reasonable wine list. 🔌 Harbourfront • 28410 41451 • Closed Nov–Apr • €€

8 Paragadi, Siteia
One of the best places for fish in Siteia, with tables overlooking the waterfront esplanade. 🔌 Karamanlis 8 • €€€

9 Porfira, Makrygialos
In the unlikely setting of cheap and cheerful Makrygialos, Porfira serves a gourmet menu of uniquely Cretan dishes, which staff are happy to guide you through. 🔌 Makrygialos • 28430 52189 • Closed Oct–May • €€€

10 Marilena, Elounda
Simply grilled fresh seafood is what Marilena does best, though it also serves other Greek dishes, created with an appealing lightness of touch. 🔌 On the harbour • 28410 41322 • Closed Nov–Feb • €€€

Marilena, Elounda

STREETSMART

Getting To and
Around Crete
116

General Information
117

Things to Avoid
118

Special Interest Holidays
119

Eating and Drinking Tips
120

Shopping Tips
121

Budget Ideas
122

Tips for Families and
the Disabled
123

Banking and
Communications
124

Health and Security Tips
125

Where to Stay
126–131

CRETE'S TOP 10

Left **Long-distance ferry** Centre **Local bus** Right **Vehicles for hire**

Getting To and Around Crete

Scheduled Flights
The only year-round way of getting to Crete is to fly to Athens and take a connecting flight to Irakleio or Chania. Easyjet flies direct from London (Gatwick) and Manchester to Irakleio in summer. Olympic and Aegean Airlines connect Crete with many other Greek islands.

Charter Flights
Charter airlines owned by large package holiday companies fly to Chania and Irakleio from most airports in the UK and large mainland EU cities in summer. The first departures are in late April or early May, with the last return flight in early October. Most flights are sold as a package with accommodation and car rental.

Ferries
Fast ferries sail overnight, every night, between Piraeus, the port of Athens, and Irakleio on Crete. There are also (less frequent) services to Chania and Rethymno. Another popular option is to island-hop, staying for a few nights on one or more of the Cyclades.

Car Hire
There are local and international car rental companies at every airport, resort and major town in Crete. Renting on the spot is often more expensive than booking in advance with a major firm. Drive defensively and cautiously at all times – Greece has one of the worst accident rates in Europe.

Buses
Local buses operated by the KTEL consortium are a cheap and cheerful way to see Crete and meet local people. Tickets are cheap and there are regular departures even to remote villages. English-language timetables are usually available from local tourist offices.

Taxis
Taxis are surprisingly affordable, and operate not only in towns but on long journeys between towns and villages. Short journeys are metered, but for longer trips there is usually a fixed price – agree it before setting off. Most drivers speak some English, and vehicles are usually modern Mercedes saloons.

Local Boats
The only way to travel between Sougia and Chora Sfakion on the south coast is by boat. In summer, small boats putter along at least once a day, calling at Agia Roumeli and Loutro.

Riding
Mule or pony trekking is a great way to explore the awesome mountain scenery of the Lefka Ori (White Mountains), where there are still few motor roads.

Bicycle
Away from the north coast and its busy highway, there are hundreds of miles of farm tracks and jeep roads which are ideal mountain-biking territory. Cycling is best enjoyed in spring (April–May) and autumn (late September–October).

Motorbikes and Scooters
Two-wheeled transport is popular with summer visitors. However, great caution should be used, both on busy roads and off-track. Helmets are compulsory only for riders of larger motorcycles outside town limits, but should be worn at all times *(see also p118)*.

Directory

Airports
*Chania 28210 83800
• Irakleio 28103 97800*

Airlines
Aegean Air 21062 61000, www.aegeanair. com • Hellas Jet www.hellas-jet.com • Olympic 0871 2000 500, www.olympicair lines.com

Ferries
www.ferries.gr

Buses
http://bus-service-crete-ktel.com

Left **Local tourist information centre** Centre **Sign about etiquette** Right **Locked church**

🔟 General Information

1 When To Go
December, January and February are cold, wet and windy with heavy snow on the mountains. Spring flowers begin to appear in March, but sunbathing is not a real option until April, and rain is possible until May. Temperatures start to climb seriously in June, peaking at 35°C or higher in July. October can be beautiful, with sunny days and cool nights, and even November can be a good month for sightseeing, though not for the beach. Most accommodation closes between Nov–Mar.

2 Passports and Visas
UK visitors require a passport; most other EU nationals require only a valid identity card. Citizens of the USA, Canada, Australia and New Zealand do not require visas for a stay of up to 90 days.

3 Customs
Visitors from other EU countries are not subject to customs formalities. Unauthorized export of antiquities and works of art is a serious offence. If bringing prescription drugs with you, also bring a copy of the prescription and, if possible, a letter from your doctor to say why you need them.

4 Tourist Offices Abroad
The Greek National Tourism Organisation, also known as the Hellenic Tourist Organisation and referred to by its Greek acronym, EOT, has offices in all European capitals, major US cities, and in Australia and South Africa.

5 Tourist Offices in Crete
EOT has offices in Irakleio, Chania and Rethymno. There are also local tourist offices in the major resorts. All have English-speaking staff who can provide maps, bus timetables, and lists of places to stay and things to see. Most will also help you to find accommodation.

6 Opening Hours
Opening hours on Crete are erratic. Use the times given in this book as a rough guide only. Most state-run museums and archaeological sites are open around 8:30am–3pm and close on Mondays. Some may reopen or stay open to 7 or 8pm in summer. Monasteries, convents and churches are generally open during daylight hours but close for two to three hours in the afternoon. Some smaller churches may be locked: the key is usually held in the nearest village shop or *kafeneion*.

7 Etiquette
Speaking even a few words of the language often works wonders in establishing a rapport with Cretans. Modest clothing (long trousers for men, over-the-knee skirts for women) is required when visiting monasteries and churches. Topless sunbathing is generally tolerated, but nude bathing is restricted to designated beaches.

8 Electricity
Greece uses the standard European 220V/50Hz AC electrical supply. Plugs have two round pins.

9 Clothing
A sun-hat and sunglasses are essential. In spring and autumn, a light wool sweater or fleece and a light windproof and waterproof jacket are useful. Good walking boots are a must for serious hiking.

10 Useful Accessories
A small torch is good in places with little street lighting. Take at least a litre of water if you plan even an easy walk. Mosquito repellents are supplied in most guesthouses. A snorkel and mask, and compact binoculars are handy if you want to observe wildlife.

Directory

Tourist Info Line
171

GNTO
www.gnto.gr • See also pp12, 18 & 22

Streetsmart

Left **Sea urchins** Centre **Motorbikes and scooters** Right **Sun without shade**

🔟 Things to Avoid

Sunburn
1 Never underestimate the burning power of the Cretan sun, which can be punishing as early as April. Use a high-factor sunscreen or sunblock, especially on boat trips, when the sea breeze can make it seem deceptively cool, and take to the shade from midday until late afternoon.

Heatstroke
2 Heatstroke is another risk in high summer. Do not attempt strenuous hiking or mountain riding in July or August, drink plenty of water and wear a hat. Symptoms can be aggravated by alcohol – drink an exra half litre of water for each unit of alcohol you consume.

Mosquitoes
3 A night-time pest in many parts of Crete, mosquitoes breed in ponds, streams and cisterns. Out of doors, they can be kept away by deterrents containing diethyltoluamide ("deet") or the organic citronella oil. Indoors, use an electrical deterrent pad, sold in shops all over Crete.

Sea Urchins
4 Spiky black sea urchins infest most rocky beaches and can inflict a painful wound if stepped on in bare feet. Watch where you walk in shallow water. The spines, which snap off in the wound, can be pulled out with tweezers.

Jellyfish
5 Jellyfish, called *tsouchtres* in Greek, occasionally infest Cretan beaches. Most are harmless but some can inflict a painful sting. Rinsing with vinegar or a mild ammonia solution is an effective remedy, and an antihistamine tablet and cream will also reduce inflammation.

Snakes
6 Crete has numerous snakes, most of which are completely harmless and none of which have a lethal bite (though the adder, rarely seen sunbathing on sunny rocks in the mountains, has a venomous bite). Most Greek villagers will kill any snake, venomous or not, on sight, and all Cretan snakes will flee when humans approach.

Renting a Motorbike
7 Many visitors with no previous experience of riding a motorbike or scooter rent a cheap and cheerful two-wheeler, and each year brings its crop of accidents. Riding in Crete is risky, even for experienced bikers. The inexperienced should stick to four wheels. If you must rent a bike, wear a helmet at all times. Wear long trousers and a jacket, which give you a bit more protection than shorts and T-shirt if you do take a tumble.

Kamakis
8 The native male *kamaki* ("harpooner") is a summer phenomenon. These amateur gigolos are convinced that female visitors are intent on an authentic Greek holiday romance, and are more than happy to supply it. Most will take a firm "no" for an answer.

Hornets
9 These large, red and black cousins of the wasp inflict a very painful sting and should not be handled or provoked. They are often seen hovering around pools of water or drinking fountains, but will not attack if left alone.

Photographing Military Installations
10 Greek authorities are extremely sensitive on issues of national security, as a group of British plane-spotters discovered in 2002, when they were arrested and convicted of espionage after taking photographs of Greek Air Force warplanes. Do not take photographs of military airfields (which often adjoin civil airports), army bases or radar installations (which are dotted around Crete's coasts and mountains), or naval vessels (even in civil harbours), or you are likely to be charged with spying. Prohibited sites are signposted with the symbol of a camera barred by a red stripe.

Left **Cycling** Centre **Windsurfing** Right **Cruise ship**

10 Special Interest Holidays

1 Archaeology
The ancient palace sites and ruined cities of Minoan and Hellenistic Crete can be confusing without a guide. Escorted tours featuring in-depth exploration of Knosos and other sites, with guest experts and slide shows, are offered by several companies.

2 Wildlife and Ornithology
The best times to seek out Crete's people-shy animals are spring and autumn, when specialist eco-tourism operators offer wildlife and walking holidays in Sfakia and the Mt Idi range.

3 Walking and Hiking
Crete's highest mountains offer some of Europe's most inspiring wilderness walking, but can be lethal to inexperienced or lone walkers. Small group treks led by experienced guides can be safer.

4 Riding
Pony or mule-riding expeditions through the Cretan countryside and into the Lefka Ori are a new development.

5 Cycling
A number of specialist companies offer accompanied cycling holidays in Crete, usually in spring and autumn, when it's not too hot for comfort, with most of your luggage travelling ahead of you by minibus each day and back-up transport available if the going gets too tough.

6 Painting
Spring is the most popular time for painting holidays in Crete, when the clear light and multi-coloured blaze of wild flowers provide inspirational subject matter. Some painting holidays can be combined with tours of archaeological sites and wildlife areas.

7 Music and Dance
Cretans are justifiably proud of their rich, living heritage of traditional music and dance, and eager to share it with visitors. A growing number of holidays, usually with accommodation in village homes, enable you to learn some of the complicated dances.

8 Windsurfing
The strong summer breezes which spring up most afternoons make Cretan coasts ideal for windsurfing. Most major tour operators offer packages with windsurfing coaching at major resorts such as Georgioupoli and Chersonisos.

9 Diving
Scuba diving is another burgeoning pastime in Crete. Many wrecks lie in shallow waters not far offshore, and visibility is excellent. Most ancient shipwrecks are off-limits to divers, but there are plenty of wartime wrecks to explore.

10 Cruising and Island-Hopping
Cruise vessels from a number of major cruise lines call at Cretan ports including Chania and Rethymno as part of itineraries which also include ports of call on the mainland and other islands. Multi-centre island hopping holidays including a stay in Crete are also offered by some specialist companies.

Specialist Tours

Diktynna Travel
Archontaki 6, Chania • *28210 41458 (escorted tours of museums, ancient sites and areas of natural beauty)* • *www. diktynna-travel.gr*

Dolphin Diving
Hotel Rethymno Mare, Scaleta • *28310 71703*

Olympic Bike Travel
Adelianos Kampos, Rethymno • *28310 72383* • *www.olympic bike.com*

EcoGreece
1-877 838 7748 (California, USA) • *www.ecogreece.com*

Headwater Holidays
The Old School House, Chester Rd, Northwich, Cheshire, UK • *01606 720033 (guided walks and bird-watching)*

Streetsmart

Left **Traditional café** Centre **Raki bottles** Right **Café-bar, Agios Nikolaos**

Eating and Drinking Tips

Traditional Cafés
The old-fashioned *kafeneion* is a hub of village and town life, where local men gather to play backgammon and talk politics. They usually serve only Greek coffee, *frappé* (iced coffee), *ouzo* and *raki*, Greek brandy, bottled beer and a limited range of soft drinks.

Ouzeris and Mezedopoleion
These are the Greek equivalent of the Spanish tapas bar, serving *ouzo*, wine, beer and a range of snacks *(meze)* to accompany your drink. In a *mezedopoleion* you can order a complete meal of a dozen tiny dishes.

Pastry Shops
The *zacharoplasteion* (patisserie) is evidence of the Greek love of all things sweet. You will find honey-soaked baclava and an array of pastries stuffed with raisins and nuts and powdered with sugar and cinnamon, cream-filled pies and chocolate gateaux. The *zacharoplasteion* also serves coffee and sometimes a range of liqueurs and spirits.

Fish Restaurants
The *psarotaverna* (fish tavern) serves every imaginable kind of seafood, from tiny whitebait to whole sea bass, shrimp, octopus, squid, langouste and less familiar delicacies, including sea urchins. Fish is officially classed

category "A" (the most expensive) through "E" and is priced by weight.

Grill Restaurants
The *psitesteatoreon* or grill restaurant is a carnivore's delight and a vegetarian's nightmare. The typical menu comprises chicken, lamb and pork, spit-grilled and served with chips and salad. Less familiar dishes include *kokoretsi* (liver and other offal wrapped in intestines and grilled) and sheep's head.

Giros (Kebab) Stands
The ubiquitous *giros* (pronounced "hero") is Greece's own greasy and delicious fast food – slivers of veal, pressed into a vertical cylinder and cooked on a revolving grill, shaved off and served in flat pitta bread with onions, tomatoes, yoghurt and a dash of cayenne pepper. *Giros* stands are strategically located in most towns and larger villages.

Café-Bars
Neon-lit, gleaming new café-bars cater to holiday crowds in main resorts and to younger Greeks in towns such as Irakleio, Chania and Rethymno. They serve expensive imported lagers, iced coffee, soft drinks and disturbingly powerful cocktails, usually based on locally made vodka, tequila, rum or gin.

Raki and Wine
Tsikoudia, or *raki*, is Crete's fiery traditional tipple, and is served neat in tiny glasses, sometimes first thing in the morning with coffee. Cretans rarely drink more than one at a sitting; nor should you. Wines include pine resin-flavoured *retsina* (sold straight from the barrel or in 500 ml bottles) and drinkable red and white wines from Crete and elsewhere in Greece *(see also p71)*.

Beer
Lager beers including Amstel and Heineken are brewed under licence in Greece and sold in 500 ml bottles. Local brands including Mythos and Fix (the first beer brewed in Greece, introduced by a Bavarian brewer in the 1840s), also in 500 ml bottles. Café-bars also serve imported brands including Budweiser and Beck's. Bottled Newcastle Brown Ale, Guinness and British keg lagers on draft are served in some holiday resorts.

Water and Soft Drinks
Greek tap water is perfectly safe to drink, but many visitors and Greeks themselves prefer the taste of bottled mineral water. Virtually every resort shop has a fridge stuffed with mineral water, cola, lemonade and other soft drinks.

Left **Herbs and spices for sale** Centre **Olive oils** Right **Pottery souvenirs**

ᵗᵒᵖ10 Shopping Tips

1 Shop Opening Times

Cretan markets are busiest and best early in the morning, opening at about 7:30am Monday to Saturday, and busiest of all on Saturday mornings. Markets, and all other shops, close around midday, reopening around 5pm and staying open until at least 8pm. In resort areas, many shops are open until around 11pm in summer.

2 Tax and Allowances

Non-EU residents can reclaim Value Added Tax (VAT) on most goods by presenting the relevant receipt at Customs on departure. Non-EU travellers can also buy wines, spirits, tobacco, perfumes and other goods in duty-free shops at Chania and Irakleio airports.

3 Prices and Bargaining

Bargaining over prices is not common practice in Crete, and most ticket prices are fairly firmly fixed. That said, it never hurts to ask for the best possible price, especially in art and craft shops. Prices are often notably cheaper at the very end of the holiday season, when custom is on the wane.

4 Cash or Credit?

Most traders and shop owners (as well as restaurant and small hotel owners) prefer cash to credit cards, and usually pass on to you the percentage charged by the credit card company, which can be as much as 5 per cent.

5 Wine

Aided by modern wine-making techniques, Greek wines are coming into their own, and the vineyards of Crete are no exception. The Boutari wines are among the best, and you can buy quality wines to take home in most towns and at airports.

6 Herbs

Crete is famous for the healing and cleansing properties of its wild mountain herbs, which are gathered, dried and exported in bulk all over Greece. Take home a big bag of sage, oregano, thyme or basil, sold loose or in packages in the markets of Chania, Rethymno and Irakleio.

7 Olives and Olive Oil

Olives and olive oil have been staples of the Greek diet since ancient times, and the olive groves of Crete produce some of the best. Cold pressed virgin olive oil is the key ingredient of many dishes, and quality oil (you really can taste the difference) is much cheaper in Crete than at home.

8 Pottery

Pottery-making is a living skill on Crete: look out for prettily coloured, modern bowls, plates and cups, simple old-fashioned peasant earthenware, or copies of elaborately decorated Minoan, Classical or Hellenistic ceramics.

9 Carved Wood

Unique to Crete is the curly wooden stick carved from *prinos* wood, which is the mountain shepherd's versatile tool, used to carry burdens, discipline dogs and encourage stubborn mules. They make handsome wall decorations. You may also find attractive bowls and platters turned from hard, close-grained olive wood.

10 Icons, Antiques and Handicrafts

Original icons of saints, archangels and apostles command high prices and require an export licence – reputable dealers will assist in obtaining the necessary permissions. Good copies can be bought from specialist dealers, and from museum shops in Irakleio and Chania. Look out too for antique daggers, silver pen and tobacco cases, meerschaum pipes and flintlock pistols – but beware of fakes. Colourful woolen blankets and rugs are easy to carry home, as are beautifully embroidered textiles.

Left **Ferry** Centre **Camping sign** Right **Market food**

Budget Ideas

1 Off-Season Travel
The cost of living rockets from mid-June to early September. Accommodation, air fares to Crete, and car and scooter rental are lower in spring and autumn. The best time of all for a budget visit is early October, when the sea is still warm and there is still plenty of sun but few visitors.

2 Cheap Flights and Ferries
Flying to Athens, then travelling on to Crete by ferry can be cheaper than flying direct to Crete. At least four scheduled airlines fly daily to Athens from London alone, and there are also charter flights in summer, so fares are competitive. If coming from outside Europe, look for a cheap fare to London and a connecting flight to Athens or Crete.

3 Discounts
The longer you intend to stay in one place, the cheaper your room will be. Pensions and hotels usually offer a 10 per cent discount for three nights or more, and you may get an even better rate if staying for several weeks. Most museums and archaeological sites offer cheap admission for students and school pupils.

4 Youth Hostels
There are youth hostels in Irakleio, Chersonisos, Rethymno, Siteia and Plakias, with dormitory beds (for around one-third the cost of a cheap room) and basic kitchen facilities.

5 Camping
Camping can save you some money, with most campsites charging around half the cost of a budget room for a tent and two people. On the downside, few campsites are easy to get to using public transport, and camping means carrying a tent.

6 Working Holidays
Finding casual work picking fruit or olives is less easy than it was, as migrants from Albania and other eastern European countries provide a supply of cheap labour. Bar and restaurant work in resorts is very poorly paid (most earnings are from tips), with very long hours. If you have a degree in English you may find work teaching in a private language school. In theory, EU citizens do not need work permits.

7 Hitch-hiking
Hitching can be a good way of getting around the island (especially to out-of-the-way spots), and Cretans themselves frequently hitch-hike. Off the beaten track, where there is little traffic, you may have to wait for hours in hot sun.

8 Cheap Eats
Giros stands *(see p120)* offer the cheapest tasty hot meals in Crete. Markets are piled with inexpensive fruit in summer, and if you stick to picnicking on fruit, olives, cheese and fresh-baked bread (the healthy diet of the Cretan villager), you can live on surprisingly little. In restaurants, Greek salad (onions, cucumber, tomatoes, olives and a slab of feta cheese, drowned in oil) is a cheap meal in its own right. Fish is always the most expensive dish on any menu, and chicken and squid are usually the cheapest.

9 Drinking and Entertainment
A half-litre bottle of beer or a half-litre of wine in an old-fashioned local café is usually half the price of a smaller beer or a fancy cocktail in a smart café-bar. Admission to most discos and clubs in resorts is free, but drinks are expensive. Make the most of half-price happy hour in lively resorts like Chersonisos and Malia.

10 Resorts to Avoid
Budget travellers should avoid the purpose-built north coast resorts – including Elounda, Malia, Chersonisos, Bali and Georgioupoli – which cater to a captive market of high-spending holidaymakers.

Left **Aqua park** Centre **Car hire** Right **Family on the beach**

☶10 Families and Disabled Visitors

1 Hotels
All hotels in Crete welcome children. Most major holiday companies now feature hotels which are especially family-friendly, with facilities such as baby-sitting and activity clubs. Larger hotels used by major European holiday companies often have some rooms specifically designed for wheelchair users and for people with other disabilities.

2 Self-Catering Apartments and Villas
Small self-catering complexes are a popular family choice. Villas with pools can be ideal for families. On the down side, most villas on Crete are some distance from the beach.

3 Activities for Children
Some package holiday hotels offer a range of supervised activities for younger children. Crete also has a couple of aqua-parks, with wave pools and waterslides, close to main resorts. Older children can enjoy pedalos, sea canoes, and windsurfing at resorts.

4 Feeding Children
Children may find some Greek restaurant dishes (like fish with the head still attached) intimidating. Western-style dishes, such as spaghetti, hamburgers and chips are served in all resorts.

5 Baby Necessities
Familiar brands of baby milk, baby food and nappies for infants are available at mini-markets in the resorts, or the local *geniko emporion* (general store) or pharmacy.

6 Child Safety on the Beach
Children should wear sunblock and a hat on the beach as there is a risk of severe sunburn even as early as April. Warn children to look out for spiny black sea urchins. There are no lifeguards.

7 Cars and Buses
Rental cars are fitted with safety belts, but child seats may not be available. For short journeys use taxis rather than slow and crowded local buses. There are no disabled facilities at bus stations, but collapsible wheelchairs may be carried in the luggage compartment of long-distance buses.

8 Wheelchair Access at Airports
Unfortunately, there is not even direct wheelchair access between terminals and aircraft at Irakleio or Chania airports. Wheelchair users may even find it easier to fly to Athens and travel to Crete by ferry.

9 Wheelchair Access at Sights
Few visitor attractions or museums are fully accessible to wheelchair users, but some have ramps from street level and lifts to upper storeys. Most archaeological sites in Crete are on steep and rugged sites, with rough paths or steps and few, if any, ramps.

10 Organizations for Disabled Visitors
In the UK, organizations such as Holiday Care Service, Tripscope and RADAR provide advice on travel and accommodation in Greece for people with disabilities. Fantasy Travel organizes tailor-made holidays for people with disabilities.

Directory

Fantasy Travel
Xenofondos 8,
10557 Athens
• 2103 310530

Holiday Care Service
2nd Floor, Imperial
Buildings Victoria Rd,
Horley, Surrey, UK •
0845 1249971 • www.
holidaycare.org.uk

RADAR
12 City Forum, 250
City Rd, London EC1V
• 020 7250 3222 •
www.radar.org.uk

Disabled Holiday Directory
6 Seaview Crescent,
Goodwick, Pembroke-
shire SA64 0A2 • 0134
887 5592 585651
• www.disabledholiday
directory.co.uk

Left **Post boxes** Centre **Bank sign** Right **Telephone booth**

Streetsmart

🔟 Banking and Communications

1 Language

English is spoken more or less fluently by virtually all Cretans working in hotels, guesthouses and other tourist-related industries, and in most bars and restaurants. However, learning a few words of Greek, even if only those for "hello" *(yiassou* or *kalimera)*, "please" *(parakalo)* and "thank you" *(efkaristo)*, will be much appreciated.

2 Changing Money

Like most EU member states, Greece adopted the euro in 2002. Change money or travellers' cheques at banks in larger towns and villages, at post offices displaying a yellow "Exchange" sign, and at travel agencies and some hotels in holiday resorts. Always take your passport when changing money. Banks are normally open 8am–2pm Monday to Thursday, 8am–1:30pm Friday.

3 Credit Cards

Credit cards are widely accepted in larger hotels, more expensive shops and in some tourist restaurants, but cash is preferred in most stores, guesthouses and tavernas. Some establishments charge an additional 4–5 per cent for credit card use. You can also use your credit or debit card to withdraw euros from ATMs in all larger towns and at airports.

4 Public Phones

Phones are plentiful and efficient, with separate booths for local and international calls. International booths are prominently marked, and there are multi-lingual instructions in all phone boxes. Most use a prepaid phone card, available from most general stores and street kiosks, and this is the cheapest way of calling home. You can also use metered phones in local offices of OTE, the Greek telecommunications organization.

5 Mobile Phones

Mobiles are widely used in Greece, and European cellphone users should experience no problems in using their phones in Crete. However, coverage may be patchy in some mountain areas and in deep valleys such as the Samaria Gorge. Some US and Canadian mobile phones systems may not yet be fully compatible with Greek networks.

6 Post Offices

The post office *(taxi-dromeion)* is indicated by a round yellow sign and is usually open 7:30am–2pm Monday to Friday. Some post offices also exchange money and traveller's cheques.

7 Fax and Poste Restante

Faxes can be sent from OTE offices and from some travel agencies and hotels. Mail marked "Poste Restante" can be held for you at main post offices. You will need proof of identity to collect your mail.

8 Internet

Internet cafés with cheap broadband access are available in all main towns and resorts. Internet booking is the quickest and easiest way to book accommodation, excursions, rental cars, tours and transportation.

9 TV and Radio

The BBC World Service can be received on 9.41, 15.07 and 12.09 Mhz shortwave. Most hotels in C category (3-star) and above have satellite TV receiving Sky and CNN. Voice of America English-language broadcasts also come through clearly.

10 Newspapers

Most European newspapers can be bought in resorts the day after publicatio n. The *International Herald Tribune*, published daily, carries worldwide news and US sports reports, and includes an English edition of the main Greek daily, *Kathimerini*. For news from North America, *USA Today* is on sale in many resorts. Also published in English is the daily *Athens News*, with Greek and international reports.

Left **Cretan policeman** Centre **Medical unit** Right **Pharmacy**

Health and Security Tips

Streetsmart

1 EOT/GNTO
The EOT/GNTO organization helps tourists who encounter problems with hotels, campsites, car rental and tour companies while in Crete.

2 Travel Insurance
You should take out comprehensive travel insurance covering you for private medical treatment and for evacuation if necessary, as well as for loss or theft of belongings and expenses incurred due to delayed or cancelled flights. Make sure your policy will pay for medical and hospital fees direct and that it covers you for holiday activities such as trekking, scuba diving, riding, and motorcycling, as well as for personal liability in the event of damage to rented cars or motorcycles.

3 Minor Ailments
Sunburn and heat exhaustion and mosquito bites are easily prevented (see p118). A basic medical kit should include painkillers, anti-histamine tablets and cream for bites and stings, a diarrhoea remedy, and motion sickness tablets for boat or bus journeys.

4 Insects and Pests
Hornets, scorpions and (possibly) vipers all exist in Crete but are not dangerous unless handled. Their bites and stings are painful but not normally lethal to adults, though medical attention should be sought if small children are bitten.

5 Breakdowns and Accidents
Set up a warning triangle if possible – your hire car should be equipped with one. If anyone is injured, passers-by are required to stop and help, and you must contact the police. If involved in a collision, never admit liability, sign any statement of responsibility, or lose your temper. Contact your travel insurance company as soon as possible.

6 Doctors
There are private medical clinics in all the main towns. Many doctors speak good English. Consultations must be paid for in cash.

7 Dentists
Dentists are proficient and can be found in major towns including Irakleio, Chania, Rethymno, Agios Nikolaos, Siteia and Ierapetra. You must pay for your treatment in cash.

8 Hospitals
A European Health Insurance Card covers any necessary medical treatment for EU citizens in Greek public hospitals but it is much better to make sure your insurance covers private treatment.

9 Pharmacies
Greek pharmacists provide comprehensive advice on minor ailments and injuries, and can dispense a wide range of remedies including antibiotics, anti-inflammatories and painkillers. Most speak good English. Pharmacies (farmakia) are marked by a green cross sign.

10 Crime
Crete has a very low crime rate and is one of the safest holiday destinations in the world. However, thefts from tourists do occur. Take sensible precautions, including locking rental cars and hotel rooms, and keeping passports, tickets and spare cash in hotel safes.

Emergencies
Multilingual for all types of emergency 112
Police 100
Tourist Police 171
Ambulance 166
Fire 199
Forest fire 191
Roadside assistance 104
Coastguard 108
EOT/GNTO Contact nearest tourist office

Left **Creta Paradise** Right **Grecotel Creta Palace**

TOP 10 Luxury Resorts

1 Elounda Mare Hotel, Elounda

Undeniably the best resort hotel in Crete, the Elounda Mare is a complex of 215 suites and villas set within lush grounds. The wide variety of sports and activities include tennis and a full array of water sports, and other facilities are close by on the peninsula. ◉ *Elounda Beach, 72053 • Map N4 • 28410 41512 • www. eloundamare.gr • €€€€€*

2 Hotel St Nicolas Bay, Ag. Nikolaos

Within walking distance of the restaurants and shops of Agios Nikolaos, this is one of Crete's finest hotels. It has three swimming pools and its own semi-private beach. ◉ *72100 Agios Nikolaos • Map N4 • 28410 25041 • www.stnicolasbay.gr • €€€€€ • Closed Nov–Mar*

3 Minos Palace, Ag. Nikolaos

A highly esteemed resort of 150 rooms and bungalows close to Agios Nikolaos town. Sports facilities and several restaurants. ◉ *72100 Agios Nikolaos • Map N4 • 28410 23801 • www. mamidakishotels.gr • €€€€€ • Closed Nov–Mar*

4 Silva Maris, Limin Chersonisos

The Silva Maris has one of the finest marine spa centres in Greece, with a range of health and beauty treatments, a fine private beach and verdant gardens. ◉ *70014 Limin Chersonisos • Map L3 • 28970 22850 • www. maris.gr • €€€€€ • Closed Nov–Mar*

5 Mövenpick Resort & Thalasso

This stunning modern hotel combines traditional style and materials with up-to-date facilities and a beautiful pool. It also has a thalassotherapy spa and a sports centre. ◉ *71414 Gazi, Heraklion • Map K3 • 28103 77000 • www. moevenpick-hotels.com • €€€€€ • Closed Nov–Mar*

6 Blue Palace Resort and Spa, Elounda

Superb mix of luxury suites, bungalows and villas with spa, health centre, indoor and outdoor pools and floodlit tennis courts, plus a range of water sports. ◉ *Plakas Elounda 72100 • Map N4 • 28410 65500 • www.bluepalace.gr • €€€€€ • Closed Nov–Mar*

7 Creta Paradise, Chania

An award-winning 186-room resort on one of Crete's Blue Flag beaches, the Creta Paradise is only ten minutes away from the centre of Chania. Modern facilities include two pools, and its bungalows have been built in an attractive Neo-Classical style. ◉ *73100 Gerani • Map D2 • 28210 61315 • €€€€*

8 Out of the Blue Capsis Elite Resort

On a private headland, this five-star resort has its own private beaches, a huge pool, a choice of bars and restaurants and even its own zoo. Ideal for families, with some exclusive villas. ◉ *Agia Pelagia 71000, Irakleio • Map K3 • 2810 811112 • www.capsis.com • €€€€ • Closed Nov–Mar*

9 Grecotel Creta Palace, Rethymno

Smaller than its sister hotel the Rithymna Beach, the Creta Palace is only 4 km (2 miles) from central Rethymno, with 162 rooms in its main block and 200 bungalows and villas. It has several pools and a wide range of activities for children, as well as tennis and water sports. ◉ *74100 Missiria • Map F3 • 28310 55181 • www.grecotel.com • €€€€€ • Closed Nov–Mar*

10 Minos Beach Art 'Otel, Ag. Nikolaos

This medium-sized complex of bungalows with splendid views of the Gulf of Mirabello is set in tranquil, flower-filled gardens. Only a stroll from the centre of Agios Nikolaos, the hotel has its own sandy beaches and rocky inlets. ◉ *72100 Ag • Map N4 • 28410 22345 • www.bluegr.com • €€€€€ • Closed Nov–Mar*

  Note: *Unless otherwise stated, all hotels accept credit cards, have en-suite bathrooms and air conditioning*

Left **Mythos Suites** Right **Palazzo Rimondi**

TOP 10 Boutique Hotels

1 Mythos Suites, Rethymno

Situated in the old part of Rethymno, this smart hotel is housed in two 16th-century Venetian buildings that have been knocked into one. They surround a courtyard with a pretty pool; ground-floor rooms have verandahs adjoining the courtyard, while upper-floor rooms have wooden balconies. ⊗ C12 Plateia Karaoli, 74100 • Map F3 • 28310 53917 • www.mythos-crete.gr • €€€

2 Nostos, Chania

With a name meaning "homecoming", this little, brightly painted pension offers a friendly welcome. On a traffic-free lane in the heart of the old town, it has studio rooms with gallery beds and balconies, and fine views of the harbour from the shaded roof-top terrace. ⊗ 42–6 Zambeliou, 73113 • Map D2 • 28210 94743 • www.nostos-hotel.com • €€€

3 Palazzo Rimondi, Rethymno

Tucked away in an arcaded courtyard behind iron gates, Palazzo Rimondi is a well-restored complex of 15th-century buildings, with vaulted roofs, carved stone and wooden panelled ceilings. ⊗ 21 Xanthoudidou and 16 Har. Trikoupi, 74100 • Map F3 • 28310 51289 • www.palazzorimondi.com • €€€€ • Closed Nov–Mar

4 Casa Delfino, Chania

This 17th-century Venetian mansion, Chania's most exclusive address, has been luxuriously restored. In a quiet alley, it has fine rooftop views and the suites have been individually designed. ⊗ Theofanous 9, 73100 • Map D2 • 28210 93098 • www.casadelfino.com • €€€€€

5 Casa Leone, Chania

The "House of the Lion" has been meticulously restored, with period details such as Venetian mirrors and antique (and reproduction) furniture. The Casa Leone also has a smart cocktail bar. ⊗ Parodos Theotokopolou 18 • Map D2 • 28210 76762 • www.casa-leone.com • €€€€

6 Vecchio Hotel Apartments, Rethymno

An attractive complex, created by merging two Venetian mansions and adding a swimming pool. The hotel offers modern, well-equipped rooms and studios. ⊗ Daliani 4, 74100 • Map F3 • 28310 54985 • www.vecchio.gr • €€€ • Closed Nov–Mar

7 Lato Boutique Hotel, Irakleio

Open all year round, the Lato offers panoramic views of the Venetian Fortress and the old port of Irakleio from its modern, comfortable rooms. ⊗ 15 Epimenidou St, 71202 • Map T1 • 2810 228103 • www.lato.gr • €€€€

8 Porto del Colombo, Chania

This attractive old stone building stands close to the old harbour at Chania and, unlike some of its rivals, is open year round. There are 10 twin and double rooms, some of which have cosy gallery beds, with furnishings that harmonize with the building's traditional lines. ⊗ Theofanous and Moschon, 73131 • Map D2 • 28210 98466 • €€€

9 Villa Andromeda, Chania

Lovingly restored Neo-Classical mansion, with a lush palm garden and a large pool, elaborately painted ceilings, white marble floors, staircases and balconies. Open year round. ⊗ 150 Eleftherios Venizelou 73133 • Map D2 • 28210 28300 • www.simpsontravel.com • €€€€€ • Closed Jan–Feb

10 Suites Pandora, Chania

A stylish collection of two- and four-bed suites, some facing an inner courtyard, others looking out to sea. All have high ceilings, balconies and tall shuttered windows. ⊗ Lithinon 29, 73100 • Map D2 • 28210 43588 • www.pandorahotel.gr • €€€

Left **Nostalgia Studios** Centre **Creta Helena** Right **Anna Apartments**

Self-Catering Apartments

1 Elounda Residence, Elounda

Set in lush gardens about 20 minutes' walk from the village, this is an excellent complex, with 24-hour reception, bars, restaurant and mini-market to complement its two- to four-bed apartments. Facilities include a large saltwater pool, children's pool, tennis court and mini-golf. ✆ 72053 Elounda • Map N4 • 28410 41823 • Closed Nov–Mar • www.elounda residence.gr • €€€

2 Casa Veneta, Chania

This Venetian mansion near the harbour has been divided into double and twin-bedded studios, and open-plan apartments sleeping up to four people on three floors, with twin-bed galleries and balconies, some with sea views. ✆ Theotokopoulou 55–7, 73131 Chania • Map D2 • 28210 90007 • Closed Nov–Mar • €€€

3 Marina Studios, Malia

A modern complex of 11 apartments and studios, just 300 m from the beach and 6 km (4 miles) from the bright lights of Chersonisos. ✆ Malia 70007 • Map M4 • 28970 33370 • €€

4 Nostalgia Studios, Georgioupoli

An attractive small complex close to the village

centre. It has a small pool and choice of studios and apartments for two to four people. All have shower, kitchenette and balcony or patio. ✆ 73007 Georgioupoli • Map E3 • 28250 61400 • No credit cards • Closed Nov–Apr • €€€

5 Paul-Eva Apartments, Chersonissos

These very affordable apartments, only 1 km from the beach, come with private balconies and all the amenities you would expect plus a shared pool. ✆ 70007 Chersonissos • Map M4 • 28970 23358 • Closed Nov–Mar • €

6 Creta Helena, Chania

Modern apartment complex in a quiet area, 20 minutes' walk from the harbour. It offers open-plan apartments, each with a twin or double bedroom and a living room with sofa-bed and kitchenette. There's also a small pool. ✆ I. Sfakianaki 42, 73134 Chania • Map D2 • 28210 46722 • €€€

7 Bay View Apartments, Siteia

On the fringe of Siteia and just a few paces from the beach, the Bay View has 10 apartments, most with twin beds and sofa-bed, and all with full kitchen facilities. Each room has a balcony or

verandah. ✆ Petras, 72400 • Map Q4 • 28430 24333 • No credit cards • No air conditioning • Closed Nov–Mar • www.bayview-apartments.gr • €€€

8 Zeus's House, Lasithi

Lovely apartments and family rooms furnished in a traditional manner. Also has a swimming pool. Located in the heart of the lush Lasithi Plateau near the village of Agio Konstantinos and close to several taverns and restaurants. ✆ Agio Konstantinos, 72052 • Map M4 • 02810 222218 • www.greekhotel.com • €€€

9 Kastri Village, Palaiocastro

Between Palaiocastro and Kouremenos beach, these 32 self-catering apartments with kitchenettes, verandahs and a pool. The beach is close by. ✆ 72300 Palaiokastro • Map R4 • 28430 61100 • Closed Nov–Mar • €€€

10 Anna Apartments, Paleochora

Smothered with flowers and greenery, this attractive little complex is on a quiet side street close to the beach. All apartments have one or two bedrooms, living room, kitchen and verandah. There's also a children's play area. ✆ Paleochora • Map B4 • 28103 46428 • No credit cards • €€€

Note: Unless otherwise stated, all hotels accept credit cards, have en-suite bathrooms and air conditioning

Left **Kalives Beach Hotel** Right **Porto Loutro Hotel**

TOP 10 Beach Hotels

1 Iberostar Creta Panorama, Rethymno

Four outdoor pools, a heated indoor pool, six tennis courts, sauna and water sports that include scuba diving make this huge beach resort one of the best hotels in Crete for an active holiday. Accommodation is in suites or bungalows.
⊗ *Panormo • Map F3 • 28340 51512 • Closed Nov–Mar • €€€€€*

2 Kalives Beach Hotel, Kalives

Situated between two sandy beaches on Souda Bay, this hotel overlooks the river and has 150 rooms in two wings, each with a pool. There is an attractive riverside terrace restaurant and easy beach access. ⊗ *7303 Kalives • Map E2 • 28250 31285 • Closed Nov–Mar • www.kalyvesbeach.com • €€€€*

3 Aegean Palace Hotel, Platanias

Fields separate this low-rise hotel from the nearby beach. Its rooms surround a large pool (with poolside bar) and some suites have their own small pools. Other facilities include a gym, sauna, tennis court and playground. ⊗ *73014 Kontomari, Platanias • Map C2 • 28210 62668 • Closed Nov–Mar • €€€€*

4 Porto Loutro Hotel, Loutro

This very attractive hotel just above the beach at

Loutro has 36 rooms (plus four self-catering studios). They are in two buildings in separate parts of this village, set among palm trees, bougainvillea and tamarisk. It is accessible only by boat.
⊗ *73011 Loutro, Anopoli • Map D4 • 28250 91433 • No credit cards • Closed Nov–Feb • www.hotelportoloutro.com • €€*

5 Aquila Hotel & Resorts, Rethymno

Aquila Elounda is exclusively for adults, offering luxury rooms overlooking Mirabello Bay. There are also two beach resorts a short walk from Rethymno. ⊗ *74100 Rethymno • Map F3 • 28310 71002 • www.aquilahotels.com • €€€€*

6 Astir Beach Hotel, Gouves

This hotel overlooks a fine, sandy beach and has two pools, a tennis court and a range of other land and water sports, including a scuba diving centre. It also has a children's playground.
⊗ *70014 Gouves • Map L3 • 28970 41141 • Closed Nov–Mar • €€€€*

7 Louis Creta Princess Club, Maleme

Built around a complex of lagoon-like swimming pools on the beach at Maleme Bay, this tropical-style resort offers tennis, football, archery, mini-golf and basketball.

⊗ *73100 Maleme • Map C2 • 28210 62702 • Closed Nov–Mar • €€€€*

8 Neos Alianthos Garden Hotel, Plakias

Across the road from one of Crete's best beaches, this family-run hotel is the best in Plakias. It has a children's pool, freshwater pool and pool-bar, a supermarket and restaurant. ⊗ *74060 Plakias • Map F4 • 28320 31280 • Closed Dec–Feb • www.alianthos.gr • €€€*

9 Athina Palace, Irakleio

A large beach hotel with three outdoor pools and its own beach. Accommodation comes in a choice of two- or three-person bungalows, family bungalows sleeping two adults and two children, and four-person maisonettes with sea view.
⊗ *71001 Agia Pelagia • Map K3 • 28108 11800 • Closed Nov–Mar • €€€€€*

10 Rethymno Mare Royal

Opened in 2001 at Scaleta, 11 km (7 miles) east of Rethymno, the Rethymno Mare Royal has landscaped gardens and a pool, a restaurant, three bars and its own nightclub. It also offers a range of water sports, including a diving school.
⊗ *74100 Rethymno • Map F3 • 28310 72640 • Closed Nov–Mar • www.rethymnomare.com • €€€€€*

Left **Milia Village** Centre **Aphrodite, Sougia** Right **The Blue House**

Village Guesthouses

1 Milia Village
Set in the forested slopes of Crete's "wild west", Milia offers 13 rooms in village houses rebuilt between 1982 and 1993 in local stone and wood. The rooms are heated by wood-burning stoves, while water comes from mountain springs.
Ⓢ 73012 Milia, Vlatos
• Map B3 • 28210 46774
• No air conditioning
• www.milia.gr • €€

2 Parthenagogio, Chania
A chance to live like Cretan villagers, helping with wine-making, olive picking, herding goats, basket weaving and baking. A co-operative venture, Parthenagogio was restored by villagers in the mid-1990s and now has its own taverna, serving Cretan dishes and wines from its own vineyards. Ⓢ Apokoronas
• Map D2 • 28250 23050
• No credit cards • No air conditioning • €€€

3 Aspros Potamos, Makrygialos
A settlement of 10 adobe-style cottages for lovers of the simple life, with water from the well and paraffin lamps for lighting (though bathroom lights and fridges in each house use solar energy).
Ⓢ Aspro Potamos, Makrygialos, 72055 Ierapetra
• Map P5 • 28430 51694
• No credit cards • No air conditioning • www.aprospotamos.com • €

4 White River Cottages, Makrygialos
This group of shepherds' cottages with stone floors, low wooden ceilings and corner fireplace nooks stands in groves of pine, olive and carob trees. The sandy beach at Makrygialos is less than 2 km (1 mile) away, and there is a tiny swimming pool on site. Ⓢ Aspros Potamos, Makrygialos 72055, Ierapetra
• Map P5 • 28430 51120
• No air conditioning • €€€

5 Aphrodite, Sougia
Pretty pension in a quiet, leafy lane just off Sougia's somnolent main street. Clean, affordable rooms with blue-painted balconies, marble-topped tables and lots of flowers.
Ⓢ Sougia • Map C4 • 28230 51414 • No credit cards
• No air conditioning • €€

6 Arolithos, Tylissos
A complex of stone houses with an array of traditional crafts, from pottery and icon painting to basket weaving and embroidery. Traditional music and dance performed nightly. Ⓢ Arolithos, 71500 Servili, Tylissos • Map J4 • 28108 21050 • www.arolithos.com • €€€

7 The Blue House, Loutro
Amiable guest house, with balconies overlooking the bay and the slopes of the White Mountains. Particularly handy as an overnight stop on the way to or from Agia Roumeli and the Samaria Gorge.
Ⓢ Loutro • Map D4 • 28250 91127 • No credit cards
• No air conditioning • €€

8 Spinalonga Village, Elounda
Coastal Spinalonga Village is a group of traditional-style stone houses beside the Gulf of Mirabello, with views across to Spinalonga, and shops and places to eat at Plaka village (a five-minute walk). Ⓢ 72053 Elounda
• Map N4 • 28410 41494/6
• No air conditioning
• €€€€€

9 Koutsounari Cottages, Ierapetra
Hillside holiday village above the Libyan Sea, with a choice of restored stone cottages, with modern kitchens and bathrooms, or fully up-to-date studios. All have verandahs or tiny gardens, and there is a pool, snack bar and taverna next door.
Ⓢ 72200 Ierapetra • Map N6 • 28420 61815 • Some air conditioning • www.traditionalcottages.gr • €€€

10 Diktaeon Andron, Psychro
A tiny guesthouse in Psychro village that makes a good base for a visit to the Diktian Cave or for exploring the Lasithi Plateau, high in the mountains of eastern Crete. Ⓢ 72052 Psychro, Lasithi • Map M4 • 28440 315 04 • No credit cards
• No air conditioning • €

Note: Unless otherwise stated, all hotels accept credit cards, have en-suite bathrooms and air conditioning

Left **Hamam House** Right **Metohi Kindelis**

TOP 10 Villas

1 Elounda Gulf Villas

Crete's most luxurious villa complex has 18 villas and 10 suites, each with private pool. All have washing machines and dishwashers, and marble bathrooms with whirlpool tubs. Fine sea views are to be had; on fine days right across the Gulf of Mirabello. ✿ *72053 Elounda • Map N4 • 28410 90300 • www.eloundavillas.com • Closed Nov–Mar • €€€€€*

2 Villa Dafnes, Dafnes

This stunning three-bedroom, 19th-century house in the heart of Crete's top wine region has a flower-filled courtyard, open-plan kitchen and dining room, and an eight-metre swimming pool. The price includes car hire. ✿ *Dafnes • Map J4 • Reservations Inntravel (00 44) 1653 617755 • www.inntravel.co.uk • €€€€€*

3 Villa Iason, Maleme

Three villas, each with its own pool, share a larger pool with two apartments in a Mediterranean-style mansion. Other shared facilities include a gym, sauna, plunge pool and wine cellar. Fully serviced, with a cook on request. ✿ *73100 Maleme • Map C2 • Reservations Imagine Crete 28210 99324 • www.imaginecretehotels.com • €€€€€*

4 Villa Christina, Almirida

On a hilltop above Almirida beach, with a superb pool and views over Souda Bay. A double room, two twins, fully equipped kitchen and maid service. Also with a wonderful sea-facing terrace. ✿ *Plaka, Almirida • Map D2 • Reservations Holidaylets (00 44) 1234 756940 • www.holidaylets.net • Closed Nov–Mar • €€€€*

5 Footscapes of Crete, Rethymno

There are wonderful views of the sea and mountains from these modern villas in the quiet village of Kastellos. Guided country walks are offered. ✿ *Kastellos, Rethymno • Map F3 • 69749 94598 • www.footscapesofcrete.com • €€€€€*

6 Hamam House, Vamos

This dinky villa, once part of a Turkish pasha's villa, has a small pool and garden. It is in a delightful old village, but the bright lights of Chania are only half an hour away. Ideal for a couple. ✿ *Vamos • Map E3 • Reservations www.greekislandsclub.com • (00 44) 20 8232 9780 • Not available Nov–Mar • €€€€€*

7 Vamos Houses, Vamos

Luxury in this village of restored traditional buildings, with a private courtyard and balcony. ✿ *Vamos • Map E3 • 28250 23251 • www.vamossa.gr • €€€*

8 Villa Stratos, Kalonyktis

A three-villa complex surrounded by flower- and fruit-filled gardens. The villas vary in size and two have their own pools. The pretty village of Kalonyktis, with its mini-market and taverna, is a short walk away. ✿ *Kalonyktis • Booking through Stratos Villas 28310 26956 • Closed Nov–Mar • No credit cards • www.stratosvillas.com • €€€*

9 Metohi Kindelis, Chania

Two villa apartments, each with its own garden and pool, within a huge family farmhouse dating from Venetian times. It is surrounded by apricot and orange groves, and a huge lawn. Inside, are cool marble floors and modern facilities. ✿ *Pervolia, Chania • Map D2 • 28210 41321 • No air conditioning • No credit cards • www.metohi-kindelis.gr • €€€€€*

10 Avdou, Lasithi

Set in the grounds of a small organic farm where fruit trees grow on the Lasithi slopes. There are six apartments, all with shower, kitchen, dining room, and living room. ✿ *70005 Avdu Pediados • Map M4 • 28103 00540 • www.avdou.com • €€€*

General Index

Page numbers in **bold**
type refer to main entries.

A

accidents 125
accommodation 126–31
Acropolis (Kastro), Gortys
25
Adoration of the Magi
(Damaskinos) 57
Aegean Palace Hotel,
Platanias 129
Agia Galini 44, 75, 86
Agia Roumeli, Samaria
Gorge 27, 52
Agia Roumeli-Chora
Sfakion boat trip 46
Agia Roumeli-Loutro walk
52
Agia Triada 34, 81
Agia Triada Sarcophagus,
Irakleio Archaeological
Museum 14
Agioi Deka (Ten Saints) 63
Agios Eftihios (St
Eustacius) 63
Agios Georgios (St
George) 63
Agios Ioannis Prodromos
(St John the Baptist) 63
Agios Ioannis Theologos
(St John the Divine) 63
Agios Michalis (St
Michael) 63
Agios Nikolaos (St
Nicholas) 63
Agios Nikolaos 62, 74, 103
Agios Pavlos (St Paul) 63
Agios Pavlos beach 27, 98
Agios Titos (St Titus) 63
Akrotiri Peninsula 99
Alikianos 49
Amari Valley 7, **28–9** *see
also* Mt Idi
Amari village 29
Amnesia, Kato Zakros 112
Ancient Knosos 6, **8–9**, 11,
34, 79, 80
ancient sites 34–5
Andikithira 47
Anna Apartments,
Paleochora 128
Anna Bei 1900, Iarapetra
73, 112
Anogeia 99

antiques 121
Aphroditem, Sougia 130
Apicorno Café, Kalives 72
Aptera 99
Aquapark, Chersonisos 47
Aquila Hotel & Resorts,
Rethymno 129
archaeologists 10–11
Archaia Eleftherna 99
Archive, Phaestos 21
Argyroupoli 48
Arkadiou 62
Armida Boat Club, Agios
Nikolaos 112
Arolithos, Tylissos 130
Aroma, Chania 72
askomandoura 61
Aspros Potamos 51
Aspros Potamos,
Makrygialos 130
Astir Beach Hotel, Gouves
129
Athina Palace, Irakleio 129
Avdou, Lasithi 131
Avli, Rethymno 68, 101
Axos 48

B

babies 123
baglamas 61
Bali 45, 86
banking 124
bargaining 121
Barko Café, Agios Nikolaos
72
bars *see* cafés, bars and
ouzeries
Bay View Apartments,
Siteia 128
beaches and beach resorts
Central Crete 86
Eastern Crete 110
Top Ten 44–5
Western Crete 98
beer 120
Blue House, The, Loutro 130
Blue Palace Resort and
Spa, Elounda 126
boat trips 46–7, 116
Boutari Winery, Archanes
64, 81
bouzouki 60
Boyd-Hawes, Harriet 10, 13
Bronzesmith's workshop,
Gournia 31
budget travel 122

Bull from the Sea, The
(Renault) 57
Bull's Head Rhyton,
Irakleio Archaeological
Museum 15
buses 116, 123
Byzantine Empire 32, 33

C

Café du Lac, Agios
Nikolaos 112
Café Zygos, Agios
Nikolaos 112
cafés, bars and ouzeries
120
Central Crete 88
Eastern Crete 112
Top Ten 72–3
camping 122
car hire 116, 123
Carpenter's workshop,
Gournia 31
Casa Delfino, Chania 127
Casa Leone, Chania 127
Casa Veneta, Chania 128
castles 40–41
catamaran sailing 47
Cave of the Holy Fathers
59
caves 59, 104
Central Court, Ancient
Knosos 8
Central Court, Phaestos
20
Central Crete 78–89
bars and cafés 88
beaches 86
map 78
restaurants 89
Central Palace Court,
Gournia 30
Chania 6, **18–19**, 74, 91
Chania Castle 40
cheeses 66
Chelidon, Elounda 113
Chersonisos 74, 86
Chestnut Festival 62
children 123
Chionia 110
Chora Sfakion 63, 99
Chrysi 47

churches
  Agia Anna, Axos 48
  Agia Ekaterini, Irakleio 82
  Agia Irene, Kournas 48
  Agia Paraskevi, Topolia 49
  Agioi Deka 43
  Agios Eftihios, Hromonastiri 29
  Agios Frangiskos, Rethymno 94
  Agios Georgios, Kournas 48
  Agios Georgios, Voila 49
  Agios Ioannis, Alikianos 49
  Agios Ioannis Theologis, Kardaki 29
  Agios Mikhail Arkhangelos, Asomatos 87
  Agios Nikolaos, Agios Nikolaos 103
  Agios Nikolaos, Chania 43
  Agios Nikolaos, Samaria Gorge 26
  Agios Titos, Irakleio 83
  Basilica of Agios Titos, Gortys 24
  Osia Maria, Samaria Gorge 27
  Panagia, Thronos 29
  Panagia Kera 42
  Tessaron Martyron, Rethymno 94
  Top Ten 42–3
Ciao, Irakleio 88
Classical Temple, Phaestos 21
clothing 117
Courtyard, Gournia 30
crafts, traditional 39, 121
credit cards 121, 124
Creperie Mike, Siteia 112
Creta Helena, Chania 128
Creta Paradise, Chania 126
Cretan Handicraft, Mirthios 65
Cretan Journal (Lear) 57
Cretan sausages (loukanika) 66
Cretaquarium, Irakleio 87
crime 125
cruising and island-hopping 119

customs 117
cycling 116, 119

D
Da Molini Castle Ruins, Alikianos 41
Dalianis, Chatzimichalis 32, 57
Damaskinos, Michael 57
Damnoni 98
Daskalogiannis, Ioannis 32, 56
dentists 125
Dia 47
Diktaeon Andron, Psychro 130
Diktian cave 58, 59, 80
Diktian cave walk 53
diouli 61
Disabled Holiday Directory 123
disabled visitors 123
discounts 122
diving 119
doctors 125
Dolphin Frescoes, Ancient Knosos 8
Dorians 33
duty-free allowances 121
Dytikos (Lendas) 86

E
E4 European Mountaineering Footpath 53
Easter 62
Eastern Crete 102–113
  bars and cafés 112
  beaches 110
  map 102
  places to eat 113
El Greco 12, 56, 57
El Greco Museum 37
Ela, Chania 68, 101
Elafonisi 46, 50, 98
Electra Restaurant, Stalida 89
electricity 117
Elos 49, 62
Elounda 104
Elounda Mare Hotel, Elounda 69, 113, 126
Elounda Gulf Villas 131
Elounda Residence, Elounda 128

emergencies 125
EOT (Greek National Tourism Organisation) 117, 125
Epiphany 63
Epohes (Four Seasons Bar), Chania 100
Erotokritos, Ammoudara 89
Erotokritos (Kornaros) 57
Ethia 49
etiquette 117
Etz Hayyim Synagogue, Chania 19
Evans, Sir Arthur 8, 9, 10, 11

F
Falasama 98
families 123
Fantasy Travel 123
faxes 124
Feast of the Annunciation 63
ferries 116, 122
Festival of Agios Titos 63
Festival of St Nicholas, Agios Nikolaos 62
Festival of the Virgin Mary 62
festivals 62–3
Firkas, Chania 18
First Palace remains, Phaestos, 21
fish 69
fish restaurants 120
flights 116, 122
food and drink 66–7, 120, 122
Footscapes of Crete 131
Fortetza, Chania 72
Four Lions, The, Irakleio 88
Fourfouras 29
Frangokastello 40, 59, 92

G
gaming board, Irakleio Archaeological Museum 15
Gavdos 46
Georgioupoli 44, 93
gerakokoudouna 60
Gigilos and Volakia Peaks 26
giros 120

Glika Nera (Sweetwater beach) 98
Gortys 7, **24–5**, 34, 59, 79
Gournia 7, **30–31**, 34, 106
Gramvoussa Peninsula 99
Grand Stairway, Phaestos 20
Great Staircase, Ancient Knosos 9
Grecotel Creta Palace, Rethymno 126
Greek coffee (kafe elliniko) 67
Greek Islands Club 119
grill restaurants 120
guesthouses 130

H
Hadzidakis, Joseph 10
Halbherr, Federico 10, 20
Hall of Double Axes, Ancient Knosos 9
Hall of Frescoes, Irakleio Museum 14
Hamam House, Vamos 131
Hamezi 49
Hania see Chania
haniotis 61
harbour, Rethymno 23, 95
Hard Rock Café, Chersonisos 88
hasapikos 61
Headwater Holidays 119
health tips 125
heatstroke 118
Hellas, Elounda 112
Herakleion see Irakleio
herbs 67, 121
Hersonisos see Chersonisos
history 32–3
hitch-hiking 122
Holiday Care Service 123
hornets 118
hospitals 125
Hotel St Nicolas Bay, Agios Nikolaos 126
hotels 123
   beach hotels 129
   boutique hotels 127
   luxury resorts 126
Hromonastiri 29

I
I Erganos, Irakleio 89
Iberostar Creta Panorama, Rethymno 129

Ibrahim Han Mosque, Rethymno 22
icons 121
Idaian cave 28, 59
Ierapetra 105, 107
Ilithia cave 59
Imbros Gorge 51, 52
Imeri Gramvousa 47
Inatos grotto 59
Independence Day 63
insurance 125
internet 124
Irakleio 6, **12–13**, 75, 80, 82–3, 86
Irakleio Archaeological Museum 6, 12, **14–15**, 36
islands 46–7
Istro 110
Itanos 35, 111
Itanos, Agios Nikolaos 71
Itzedin Fort, Aptera 41

J
jellyfish 118
jet skiing 47
Jug of Reeds, Irakleio Archaeological Museum 15

K
Kafeneio, Matala 88
Kafeneion O Minares, Rethymno 100
Kafeneion Yannis, Paleochora 100
Kali Kardia, Siteia 73
Kalives Beach Hotel 129
Kalliontzis, Koutsouras 113
Kaloi Limenes 86
Kalokairinos, Minos 11
kamakis 118
Kamares cave 29, 59
Kanakakis, Lefteris 57
Kandanoleon, Georgios 41
Kapetaniana 53
Kariatis, Chania 68, 101
Karnagio, Chania 68, 101
Kastelli Kissamou 93
Kastri Village, Palaiocastro 128
Kato Gouves (Gouvia) 86
Kato Zakros 110
Kavouri, Limin Chersonisos 70
Kazantzakis, Nikos 56, 57, 81
Kipouli, Malia 88

kithara 61
Knosos see Ancient Knosos
Komboloi 52, Chania 65
Kornaros, Ioannis 42, 57
Kornaros, Vinzentzos 57
Koufonisi 47
Koules (Venetian Fortress), Irakleio 12
Kouremenos 110
Kournas 48
Kourtaliotiko Gorge 51
Koutsounari Cottages, Ierapetra 130
Kritsa 48, 111
KTEL buses 116
Kyria Maria, Rethymno 68, 101

L
La Jetee, Paleochora 100
Lake Kournas 51
Lake Votamos (Zaros) 51
Landen Apan, Chania 65
language 124
laouta 60
Lasithi 50, 53, 80
Lato 48, 105
Lato Boutique Hotel 127
Lear, Edward 57
Lefka Ori see White Mountains
Levin 35
lighthouse, Chania 19
Limin Chersonisos 44
Lithines 107, 111
Local Products Exhibition, Farmers' Union of Siteia 64
Lord, Thou Art Great icon (Kornaros) 42, 57
Louis Creta Princess Club, Maleme 129
Loukoulos, Irakleio 89
Loutro 53, 92
lyra 60

M
Makrygialos 45, 104, 107, 110
Malia 44, 74, 86
Malia Palace 34, 87
mandinades 61
Marilena, Elounda 71, 113
Marilenna Studios and Apartments, Malia 128
markets
   Chania 18, 64

(markets cont.)
Irakleio 13, 64, 82
Rethymno 65, 94
Marmara (Marble beach) 98
Matala 24, 44, 86
Melidoni cave 59
Memorial to Peace, Nida Plateau 29
Metohi Kindelis, Chania 131
meze dishes 73
mezedopoleion 120
Milatos 110
Milia Village 130
Minoan Empire 21, 32, 33
Minoan jewellery and helmets, Irakleio Archaeological Museum 15
Minoan villa site, Tylissos 87
Minoan villa site, Vathypetrou 87
Minos, Irakleio 89
Minos, King 8, 56, 58
Minos Beach Art 'Otel, Agios Nikolaos 126
Minos Palace, Agios Nikolaos 126
Minotaur 8, 58
Mirtos 110
MoCafe, Irakleio 88
Mochlos 105, 106
monasteries
Moni Agia Irini 99
Moni Agia Triada 42
Moni Arkadiou 42
Moni Asomaton, Amari Valley 29
Moni Katholikou 43
Moni Chrissopygis 43
Moni Gonia 99
Moni Gouverneto 42, 99
Moni Kapsa 111
Moni Katholikou 99
Moni Koudouma 87
Moni Preveli 42
Moni Toplou 42, 106, 111
Moni Vaisamonerou 57
Top Ten 42–3
money 121, 124
Morosini Fountain, Irakleio 13, 83
Mosque of the Janissaries, Chania 19
mosquitoes 118
motorbikes and scooters 116, 118
Mt Giouchtas 87

Mt Idi (Psiloritis) 28, 53, 80 see also Amari Valley
Mt Kofinas 87
Mt Kofinas walk 53
Mövenpick Resort & Thalasso 126
museum shops 64
museums
Agios Nikolaos Archaeological Museum 36
Agios Nikolaos Folklore Museum 38
Archanes Collection 37, 87
Arolithos Museum of Agricultural History and Popular Art 39
Byzantine Collection, Chania 19, 36
Chania Archaeological Museum 18, 36
Cretan House Folklore Museum, Chania 19, 39
El Greco Museum, Fodele 37
Folklore and Martial Museum, Somatas 39, Gortys Museum 25
Historical and Folk Art Museum, Rethymno 22, 38, 94
Historical and Folklore Museum of Gavalochori 39
Historical Museum of Crete, Irakleio 12, 83
Ierapetra Archaeological Museum 37
Irakleio Archaeological Museum 6, 12, **14–15**, 36
Kazantzakis Museum, Mirtia 81
Lychnostasis Open Air Museum of Folk Culture, Chersonisos 38
Museum of the Battle of Crete, Irakleio 13
Museum of Cretan Ethnology, Vori 38, 87
Museum of History, Paleochora 38
Museum of Religious Art, Irakleio 13, 37
Museum of Rural Life, Piskopiana 38

(museums cont.)
Natural History Museum, Irakleio 13
Naval Museum, Chania 18
Rethymno Archaeological Museum 23, 36, 95
Siteia Archaeological Museum 36
Top Ten art and archaeological museums 36–7
Top Ten folklore museums 38–9
music 60–61, 119
Mycenaeans 33
Mythos Suites, Rethymno 127
myths and legends 58–9

N
Neos Alianthos Garden Hotel, Plakias 129
Nerandzes Mosque, Rethymno 22, 94
Neroutsiko and Riza Sikias, Samaria Gorge 26
New York, Chersonisos 88
newspapers 124
nightlife 74
Nikos Siragas, Rethymno 65
North Entrance Passage, Ancient Knossos 9
Nostalgia Studios, Georgioupoli 128
Nostos, Chania 127
Nostos Disco Bar, Paleochora 100

O
O Kyriakos, Irakleio 89
Oasis beach, Chania 19
octopus 67
Odeion, Ierapetra 112
Officers and Gentlemen (Waugh) 57
Old House Tavern, Malia 89
Old Mill, The, Elounda 69, 113
olive oil 121
olives 66, 121
opening hours 117, 121
Omalos Plateau 51
Oriental Bay, Paleochora 101
Ottoman Empire 32, 33

Index

P

Out of the Blue Capsis Elite Resort 126
Ouzeri Elisabeth, Malia 88
Ouzeri Manos, Ierapetra 112
ouzeries see cafés, bars and ouzeries

Pagopoieion, Irakleio 72
painting 119
Palace, Gournia 31
Palace Workshops, Phaestos 21
Palazzo Rimondi, Rethymno 127
Paleochora 41, 45, 75, 92
Paleochora-Agia Roumeli boat trip 46
Pallas Café, Chania 72
Panormos 86
Paradiso, Agia Galini 88
Paragadi, Siteia 113
passports 117
pastry shops 120
Paul-Eva Apartments, Chersonissos 128
Pefki Gorge 111
Pelekita cave, Kato Zakros 111
Pendlebury, John 10
pentozalis 61
Peristyle Hall, Phaestos 21
Phaestos 6, **20–21**, 34, 79
Phaestos Disc, Irakleio Archaeological Museum 14
pharmacies 125
Phokas, Nicephoros 33, 56
photography 118
Piano Nobile, Ancient Knosos 8
pidiktos 61
Plakias 44, 93
Platanias 74, 98
Plateia Venizelou, Irakleio 83
Platon, Nikolaos 10, 35
Point Bar, Chania 100
Polyrinia 99
Porta Kenouria, Irakleio 82
Porto del Colombo, Chania 127
Porto Loutro Hotel, Loutro 129
post offices 124
Poste Restante 124
Potter's workshop, Gournia 31
pottery 121

Poulis, Elounda village 113
Praetorium, Gortys 24
Praisos 35, 107, 111
Preveli (Finikas) 98
Profitis Ilias (Prophet Elijah) 63
Profitis Ilias cave 59
psarotaverna 120
Psiloritis see Mt Idi
psitesteatoreon 120
pumphouse and fountain, Irakleio 82

R

RADAR 123
radio 124
Raeck, Karen 29
raki 66, 120 see also tsikoudia
Raki Bar Pandelis, Sougia 100
rembetika 61
Renault, Mary 57
restaurants and tavernas 120
  Central Crete 89
  Eastern Crete 113
  Top Ten restaurants 68–9
  Top Ten tavernas 70–71
  Western Crete 101
Rethymno 7, **22–3**, 75, 91, 94–5
Rethymno beach 23
Rethymno Mare Royal 129
retsina 66, 71, 120
riding 116, 119
Rikos, Konstantinos 57
Rimondi Fountain, Rethymno 23, 95
rizitiko 61
Rodopou Peninsula 99
Roka Carpets, Chania 65
Roman Agora, Gortys 25
Roman Amphitheatre, Gortys 25
Roman Baths, Gortys 25
Roman Empire 32, 33
Roman Odeion and Code of Laws, Gortys 24
Rousa Eklisia 111
Royal Apartments, Phaestos 21
Royal Mare Village, Limin Chersonisos 126

S

St George's Day 63
saints 63

Samaria 27
Samaria Gorge 7, **26–7**, 52, 91
San Marco and the Loggia, Irakleio 83
Sanmichele, Michele 82
santouri 60
Schiavo Bastion and Venetian Walls, Chania 19
Schliemann, Heinrich 11
scuba diving 47
sea biscuit rides 47
sea urchins 118
Seagar, Richard 10
security tips 125
self-catering apartments and villas 123, 128, 131
Sfakia region 92
Sfendoni cave 59
shopping
  tips 121
  Top Ten markets and shopping streets 64–5
Shrine, Gournia 31
Sideresportes, Samaria Gorge 27
siganos 61
Simply Crete 119
Siteia 45, 75, 103, 106, 110
Skotino cave 59
snails (saligkaria) 67
Snake Goddess Figurines, Irakleio Archaeological Museum 15
snakes 118
snorkelling 47
Sougia 92, 98
Sougia-Agia Roumeli walk 52
sousta 61
South Portico, Ancient Knosos 9
Spinalonga 40, 46, 104
Spinalonga Village, Elounda 130
Stairway, Gournia 30
Stavros 98
Sterna tou Bloumosifi, Vamos 70, 101
Storehouses, Ancient Knosos 8
Storerooms, Gournia 31
Storerooms and Pithoi, Phaestos 21
Suites Pandora, Chania 127
Sultanina, Siteia 62
sunburn 118

Synagogi Bar, Chania 100
syrtos 61

T

Ta Dio Lux, Chania 100
Ta Douliana, Douliana 70
Ta Grousouzadika, Irakleio 89
Ta Leontaria, Irakleio 88
Tamam, Chania 68, 101
Tarra (Old Agia Roumeli), Samaria Gorge 27
Tavern Kato Zakros Bay 113
Taverna Agios Ioannis 20
Taverna Auoas, Agios Nikolaos 71
Taverna Pelagos, Agios Nikolaos 113
Taverna tou Zissi, Rethymno 70, 101
tavernas *see* restaurants and tavernas
tax 121
taxis 116
telephones 124
Temple of Isis and Serapis, Gortys 25
Temple of Pythian Apollo, Gortys 24
Thalassina, Irakleio 89
Theotokopoulos, Domenikos *see* El Greco
Throne Room, Ancient Knosos 9
Thronos 29
To Araxovoli, Rethymno 73
To Ellinikon, Rethymno 73
To Farangi, Agia Roumeli 70
To Maxairadiko, Chania 65
Top Hanas, Chania 65
Topolia 48
tour companies 119
tourist offices 117
Town Mosaic, Irakleio Archaeological Museum 15
Travellers on the Way to the Monastery of St Catherine (El Greco) 57

tsikoudia 66, 120
TV 124

U

Utopia Bar, Platanias 100

V

Vai 50, 103, 106, 110
Vamos 119
Vamos Houses, Vamos 131
Vamos Pension, Chania 130
Vareladika, Irakleio 71
Vecchio Hotel Apartments, Rethymno 127
Venetian Acropolis and Polyrinia 41
Venetian Arsenal, Irakleio 12, 83
Venetian Empire 33
Venetian Fortress, Irakleio 13, 83
Venetian Fortress (Fortetza), Rethymno 22, 40, 95
Venetian Fortress, Siteia 41
Venetian Gate (Porta Guora), Rethymno 23, 94
Venetian Loggia (Lotzia), Rethymno 23, 95
Venetian Tower, Finikas, Loutro 41
Veneto, Rethymno 68, 101
Venizelos, Eleftherios 33, 56
Veterano, Ierapetra 112
Villa Andromeda, Chania 127
Villa Christina, Almirida 131
Villa Dafnes, Dafnes 131
Villa Iason, Maleme 131
Villa Stratos, Kalonyktis 131
villas 131
visas 117
Voila 49, 111
Voskakis Workshop, Amari Valley 65
voulgari 61

W

Wace, Alan 11
walking 52–3, 119

War Cemetery 99
War of Independence 32
Wash Basins, Gournia 31
water, drinking 120
waterskiing 47
Waugh, Evelyn 57
West Courtyard and Theatre Area, Phaestos 20
Western Crete 90–101
bars and cafés 100
beaches 98
map 90
restaurants 101
wheelchair access 123
White Mountains (Lefka Ori) 50, 52, 90, 91
White River Cottages, Makrygialos 130
wildlife of Crete 54–5, 119
windsurfing 47, 119
wines 66, 71, 120, 121
wood carving 121
working holidays 122
World War II 33

X

Xerocampos 110
Xilouris Popular Art, Anogeia 65
Xyloskalo, Samaria Gorge 26

Y

yacht sailing 47
youth hostels 122
Ypsanta Selinou, Paleochora 65

Z

zacharoplasteion 120
Zakros 35, 107
Zakros Gorge 53, 104
Zeus 56, 58, 59, 87
Zeus's House, Lasithi 128
Zorba the Greek (Kazantzakis) 56, 57, 60, 61, 81
Zorbas, Siteia 70, 113

Acknowledgments

The Author
Robin Gauldie is a freelance travel writer and photographer based in the UK.

Contributions
Carol Edwards

Produced by BLUE ISLAND PUBLISHING

Editorial Director
Rosalyn Thiro

Art Director
Stephen Bere

Associate Editor
Michael Ellis

Designer
Lee Redmond

Picture Research
Ellen Root

Research Assistance
Amaia Allende

Main Photographers
Robin Gauldie,
Nigel Hicks

Index
Jane Simmonds

Fact Checkers
Michelle Crawford,
Liz and Paul Marsden

AT DORLING KINDERSLEY

Publisher
Douglas Amrine

Publishing Manager
Helen Townsend

Managing Art Editor
Ian Midson

Design and Editorial Assistance
Emma Anacootee, Jo Gardner, Victoria Heyworth-Dunne, Jacky Jackson, Maite Lantaron, Helen Partington, Marisa Renzullo, Karen Villabona, Dora Whitaker

Senior Cartographic Editor
Casper Morris

Senior DTP Designer
Jason Little

Senior Production Controller
Sarah Dodd

Picture Credits

Additional Photography
Max Alexander, Joe Cornish, Philip Gatward, Derek Hall, David Murray, Rob Reichenfeld, Clive Streeter.

The publishers would like to thank all the museums, archaeological sites, churches, monasteries, hotels, restaurants, bars, clubs, shops, galleries and other establishments for their assistance and kind permission to photograph.

Placement Key: t=top; tl=top left; tr=top right; tc=top centre; trc=top right centre; c=centre; ca=centre above; cra=centre right above; cb=centre below; cr=centre right; b=bottom; bra=bottom right above; bl=bottom left; br=bottom right; l=left

AKG, LONDON: 32tl, 33tl, 59tl; Eric Lessing 32c, 56c, 58tr, 58c; ALAMY IMAGES: Glen Allison 75clb; IML Image Grouup 72br; ANCIENT ART AND ARCHITECTURE: 57r; ARDEA: 60tc; Bob Gibbons 52tr; Pascal Goetcheluch 54tr; ARGYROPOULOS PRESS PHOTO: 60tl, 61r, 62tl, 62b, 63tl; AVLI: 68bl.

BRIDGEMAN ART LIBRARY: Fitzwilliam Museum, University of Cambridge, Pietro da Cortona's *Allegory of the Labours of Hercules* 58tl; Museo Archaeologico, Bari 8b; Musée de Petit Palais, Avignon, France, Peter of the Campana Cassoni's, *Defeat of Athens by Minos, King of Crete* (panel) 56tl; Sto Tome, Toledo, Spain, El Greco's *Self Portrait*, (detail from the *Burial of Count Orgaz*, 1586–8) 56b.

CORBIS: Yann Arthus-Bertrand 46c; CHRISTIE'S IMAGES: 32b; Gallo Images 54tl.

MARC DUBIN: 52tl, 52c.

GETTY IMAGES/HULTON ARCHIVE: Topical Press Agency 57tl.

HISTORICAL AND ART MUSEUM, RETHYMNO: 38b.

COURTESY OF KAZANTZAKIS PUBLICATIONS: 56tr.

COURTESY OF LYCHNOSTASIS OPEN AIR MUSEUM: 38c.

NHPA: Dr. Eckart Pott 54b; Karl Switak 55tl.

STEVE OUTRAM: 38tc, 50tl, 50b, 52b.

ROBERTHARDING.COM: Nelly Boyd 63r; Ken Gillham 61tl; Loraine Wison 47tl; Trevor Wood 53t.

STOCKPHOTO: 60tr/c/b, 66bl, 67tl; SYNAGOGI BAR: 100tl. TRAVEL LIBRARY: Philip Enticknap 62tr/ca.

PETER WILSON: 46b, 50tr.

All other images are © Dorling Kindersley. For further information see www.dkimages.com.

Cartography Credits
Martin Darlison (Encompass Graphics Ltd)

Crete map derived from East View Cartographic database: www.cartographic.com

Phrase Book

In an Emergency

Help!	**Voítheia!**	vo-ee-theea!
Stop!	**Stamatíste!**	sta-ma-tee-steh!
Call a doctor!	**Fonáxte éna giatró!**	fo-nak-steh e-na ya-tro!
Call an ambulance/	**Kaléste to asthenofóro/tin astynomía/tin pyrosvestikí!**	ka-le-steh to as-the-no-fo-ro/teen a-sti-no-the mía/teen pee-ro-zve-stee-kee!
the police/fire brigade!		
Where is the nearest telephone/hospital/pharmacy?	**Poú eínai to plisiéstero tiléfono/nosokomeío/farmakeío?**	poo ee-ne to plee-see-e-ste-ro tee-le-pho-no/no-so-ko-mee-o/far-ma-kee-o?

Communication Essentials

Yes	**Nai**	neh
No	**Ochi**	o-chee
Please	**Parakaló**	pa-ra-ka-lo
Thank you	**Efcharistó**	ef-cha-ree-sto
You are welcome	**Parakaló**	pa-ra-ka-lo
OK/alright	**Entáxei**	en-dak-zee
Excuse me	**Me synchoreíte**	me seen-cho-ree-teh
Hello	**Geiá sas**	yeea sas
Goodbye	**Antío**	an-dee-o
Good morning	**Kaliméra**	ka-lee-me-ra
Good night	**Kalin'ychta**	ka-lee-neech-ta
Morning	**Proí**	pro-ee
Afternoon	**Apógevma**	a-po-yev-ma
Evening	**Vrádi**	vrath-i
This morning	**Símera to proí**	see-me-ra to pro-ee
Yesterday	**Chthés**	chthes
Today	**Símera**	see-me-ra
Tomorrow	**Avrio**	av-ree-o
Here	**Edó**	ed-o
There	**Ekeí**	e-kee
What?	**Tí?**	tee?
Why?	**Giatí?**	ya-tee?
Where?	**Poú?**	poo?
How?	**Pós?**	pos?
Wait!	**Perímene!**	pe-ree-me-neh!
How are you?	**Tí káneis?**	tee ka-nees?
Very well, thank you.	**Poly kalá, efcharistó.**	po-lee ka-la, ef-cha-ree-sto.
How do you do?	**Pós eíste?**	pos ees-te?

Pleased to meet you.	**Chaíro pol'y.**	che-ro po-lee.
What is your name?	**Pós légeste?**	pos le-ye-ste?
Where is/are...?	**Poú eínai...?**	poo ee-neá?
How far is it to...?	**Póso apéchei...?**	po-so a-pe-chee?
How do I get to..?	**Pós mporó na páo...?**	pos bo-ro-na pa-o...?
Do you speak English?	**Miláte Angliká?**	mee-la-te an-glee-ka?
I understand.	**Katalavaíno.**	ka-ta-la-ve-no.
I don't understand.	**Den katalavaíno.**	then ka-ta-la-ve-no.
Could you speak slowly?	**Miláte lígo pio argá parakaló?**	mee-la-te lee-go pyo ar-ga pa-ra-ka-lo?
I'm sorry.	**Me synchoreíte.**	me seen-cho-ree teh.
Does anyone have a key?	**Echei kanénas kleidí?**	e-chee ka-ne-nas klee-dee?

Useful Words

big	**Megálo**	me-ga-lo
small	**Mikró**	mi-kro
hot	**Zestó**	zes-to
cold	**Kr'yo**	kree-o
good	**Kaló**	ka-lo
bad	**Kakó**	ka-ko
enough	**Arketá**	ar-ke-ta
well	**Kalá**	ka-la
open	**Anoichtá**	a-neech-ta
closed	**Kleistá**	klee-sta
left	**Aristerá**	a-ree-ste-ra
right	**Dexiá**	dek-see-a
straight on	**Eftheía**	ef-thee-a
between	**Anámesa / Metax'y**	a-na-me-sa/ me-tak-see
on the corner of...	**Sti gonía tou...**	stee go-nee-a too
near	**Kontá**	kon-da
far	**Makriá**	ma-kree-a
up	**Epáno**	e-pa-no
down	**Káto**	ka-to
early	**Norís**	no-rees
late	**Argá**	ar-ga
entrance	**I eísodos**	ee ee-so-thos
exit	**I éxodos**	ee e-kso-dos
toilet	**Oi toualétes /**	ee-too-a-le-tes
occupied/engaged	**Kateiliméni**	ka-tee-lee-me-nee

Note: words in bold (centre columns) are transliterated according to the system used by the Greek Government. However, this system is not used consistently throughout Crete, and visitors will encounter many variants on road signs, menus etc.

unoccupied	**Eléftheri**	e-l**e**f-the-ree
free/no charge	**Doreán**	tho-re-**an**
in/out	**Mésa/Exo**	me-sa/**e**k-so

Making a Telephone Call

Where is the nearest public telephone?	**Poú vrísketai o plisiésteros tilefonikós thálamos?**	po**o** vre**e**s-ke-teh o plee-see-**e**-ste-ros tee-le-fo-ni-k**o**s tha-la-mos?
I would like to place a long-distance call.	**Tha íthela na káno éna yperastikó tilefónima.**	tha **ee**-the-la na ka-no **e**-na ee-pe-ra-sti-k**o** tee-le-f**o**-nee-ma.
I would like to reverse the charges.	**Tha íthela na chreóso to tilefónima ston paralípti.**	tha **ee**-the-la na chre-**o**-so to tee-le-f**o**-nee-ma ston pa-ra-lep-tee.
I will try again later.	**Tha xanatilefoníso argótera.**	tha ksa-na-tee-le-fo-n**i**-so ar-g**o**-te-ra.
Can I leave a message?	**Mporeíte na tou afísete éna mínyma?**	bo-re**e**-te na too a-fee-se-teh **e**-na mee-nee-ma?
Could you speak up a little please?	**Miláte dynatótera, parakaló?**	mee-l**a**-teh dee-na-t**o**-te-ra, pa-ra-ka-lo?
Hold on.	**Periménete.**	pe-ri-m**e**-ne-teh.
local call	**Topikó tilefónima**	to-pi-k**o** tee-le-f**o**-nee-ma
OTE telephone office	**O OTE /To tilefoneío**	o O-T**E** /To tee-le-fo-nee-o
phone box/kiosk	**O tilefonikós thálamos**	o tee-le-fo-ni-k**o**s tha-la-mos
phone card	**I tilekárta**	ee tee-le-k**a**r-ta

Shopping

How much does this cost?	**Póso kánei?**	p**o**-so k**a**-nee?
I would like…	**Tha íthela…**	tha **ee**-the-la…
Do you have…?	**Echete…?**	**e**-che-tehá?
I am just looking.	**Aplós koitáo.**	a-pl**o**s kee-t**a**-o.
Do you take credit cards/ travellers' cheques?	**travellers' cheques Décheste pistotikés kártes/ travellers' cheques?**	th**e**-ches-teh pee-sto-tee-k**e**s k**a**r-tes/ travellers cheques?
What time do you open/close?	**Póte anoígete/ kleínete?**	p**o**-teh a-nee-ye-teh/ kle**e**-ne-teh?
Can you ship this overseas?	**Mporeíte na to steílete sto exoterikó?**	bo-re**e**-teh na to ste**e**-le-teh sto e-xo-te-ree k**o**?

This one.	**Aftó edó.**	af-t**o** e-d**o**.
That one.	**Ekeíno.**	e-ke**e**-no.
expensive	**Akrivó**	a-kree-v**o**
cheap	**Fthinó**	fthee-n**o**
size	**To mégethos**	to m**e**-ge-thos
white	**Lefkó**	lef-k**o**
black	**Mávro**	m**a**v-ro
red	**Kókkino**	k**o**-kee-no
yellow	**Kítrino**	ke**e**-tree-no
green	**Prásino**	pra-see-no
blue	**Mple**	bl**e**h

Types of Shop

antique shop	**Magazí me antíkes**	ma-ga-ze**e** me an-de**e**-kes
bakery	**O foúrnos**	o fo**o**r-nos
bank	**I trápeza**	ee tra-pe-za
bazaar	**To pazári**	to pa-z**a**-ree
bookshop	**To vivliopoleío**	to vee-vlee-o -po-le**e**-o
butcher	**To kreopoleío**	to kre-o-po-le**e**-o
cake shop	**To zacharo- plasteío**	to za-cha-ro-pla-ste**e**-o
cheese shop	**Magazí me allantiká**	ma-ga-ze**e** me a-lan-dee-k**a**
department store	**Polykatástima**	Po-lee-ka-ta-stee-ma
fishmarket	**To ichthyopoleío/ psarádiko**	to eech-thee-o-po-le**e**-o /psa-r**a**-dee-ko
greengrocer	**To manáviko**	to ma-n**a**-vee-ko
hairdresser	**To kommotírio**	to ko-mo-te**e**-ree-o
kiosk	**To períptero**	to pe-re**e**p-te-ro
leather shop	**Magazí me dermátina eíd**	ma-ga-ze**e** me ther-m**a**-tee-na ee**e**-thee
street market	**I laïkí agorá**	ee la-e**e**-ke**e** a-go-r**a**
newsagent	**O efimeridopólis**	O e-fee-me-ree-tho-p**o**-lees
pharmacy	**To farmakeío**	to far-ma-ke**e**-o
post office	**To tachydromeío**	to ta-chee-thro-me**e**-o
shoe shop	**Katástima y podimáton**	ka-t**a**-stee-ma ee-po-dee-m**a**-ton
souvenir shop	**Magazí me "souvenir"**	ma-ga-ze**e** meh "souvenir"
supermarket	**"Supermarket" / Yperagorá**	"Supermarket" / ee-per-a-go-r**a**

Bold letters in the pronunciation guides (right columns) indicate the stressed syllable.

tobacconist	**Eídi kapnistoú**	Ee-thee kap-nees
travel agent	**To taxeidiotikó grafeío**	to tak-see-thy-o-tee-ko gra-fee-o

Sightseeing

tourist information	**O EOT**	o E-OT
tourist police	**I touristikí astynomía**	ee too-rees-tee-kee a-stee-no-mee-a
archaeological	**archaiologikós**	ar-che-o-lo-yee-kos
art gallery	**I gkalerí**	ee ga-le-ree
beach	**I paralía**	ee pa-ra-lee-a
Byzantine	**vyzantinós**	vee-zan-dee-nos
castle	**To kástro**	to ka-stro
cathedral	**I mitrópoli**	ee mee-tro-po-lee
cave	**To spílaio**	to spee-le-o
church	**I ekklisía**	ee e-klee-see-a
folk art	**laïkí téchni**	la-ee-kee tech-nee
fountain	**To syntriváni**	to seen-dree-va-nee
hill	**O lófos**	o lo-fos
historical	**istorikós**	ee-sto-ree-kos
island	**To nisí**	to nee-see
lake	**I límni**	ee leem-nee
library	**I vivliothíki**	ee veev-lee-o-thee-kee
mansion	**I épavlis**	ee e-pav-lees
monastery	**moní**	mo-ni
mountain	**To vounó**	to voo-no
municipal	**dimotikós**	thee-mo-tee-kos
museum	**To mouseío**	to moo-see-o
national	**ethnikós**	eth-nee-kos
park	**To párko**	to par-ko
garden	**O kípos**	o kee-pos
gorge	**To farángi**	to fa-ran-gee
grave of....	**O táfos tou...**	o ta-fos too
river	**To potámi**	to po-ta-mee
road	**O drómos**	o thro-mos
saint	**ágios/ágioi/ agía/agíes**	a-yee-os/a-yee-ee/a-yee-a/a-yee-es
spring	**I pigí**	ee pee-yee
square	**I plateía**	ee pla-tee-a
stadium	**To stádio**	to sta-thee-o

statue	**To ágalma**	to a-gal-ma
theatre	**To théatro**	to the-a-tro
town hall	**To dimarcheío**	to thee-mar-chee-o
closed on public holidays	**kleistó tis argíes**	klee-sto tees aryee-es

Transport

When does the ... leave?	**Póte févgei to...?**	po-teh fev-yee to...?
Where is the bus stop?	**Poú eínai i stási tou leoforeíou?**	poo ee-neh ee sta-see too le-o-fo-ree-oo...?
Is there a bus to?	**Ypárchei leoforeío gia...?**	ee-par-chee le-o-fo-ree-o yia...?
ticket office	**Ekdotíria eisitiríon**	Ek-tho-tee-reea ee-see-tee-ree-on
return ticket	**Eisitírio me epistrofí**	ee-see-tee-ree-o meh e-pee-stro-fee
single journey	**Apló eisitírio**	a-plo ee-see-tee-reeo
bus station	**O stathmós leoforeíon**	o stath-mos leo-fo-ree-on
bus ticket	**Eisitírio leoforeíou**	ee-see-tee-ree-o leo-fo-ree-oo
trolley bus	**To trólley**	to tro-le-ee
port	**To limán**	to lee-ma-nee
train/metro	**To tréno**	to tre-no
railway station	**sidirodromikós stathmós**	see-thee-ro-thro-mee-kos stath-mos
moped	**To motopodílato/ To michanáki**	to mo-to-po-thee-la-to/to mee-cha-na-kee
bicycle	**To podílato**	to po-thee-la-to
taxi	**To taxí**	to tak-see
airport	**To aerodrómio**	to a-e-ro-thro-mee-o
ferry	**To "ferry-boat"**	to fe-ree-bot
hydrofoil	**To delfíni / To ydroptérygo**	to del-fee-nee / To e-throp-te-ree-go
catamaran	**To katamarán**	to catamaran
for hire	**Enoikiázontai**	e-nee-kya-zon-deh

Note: words in bold (centre columns) are transliterated according to the system used by the Greek Government. However, this system is not used consistently throughout Crete, and visitors will encounter many variants on road signs, menus etc.

Staying in a Hotel

Do you have a vacant room?	**Echete domátia**?	e-che-teh tho-ma-tee-a?
I have a reservation.	**Echo kánei krátisi.**	e-cho ka-nee kra-tee-see.
double room with double bed	**Díklino me dipló kreváti**	thee-klee-no meh thee-plo kre-va-tee
twin room	**Díklino me dipló kreváti**	thee-klee-no meh mo-na kre-vat-ya
single room	**Monóklino**	mo-no-klee-no
room with a bath	**Domátio me mpánio**	tho-ma-tee-o meh ban-yo
shower	**To douz**	To dooz
porter	**O portiéris**	o por-tye-rees
key	**To kleidí**	to klee-dee
room with a sea view/balcony	**Domátio me théa sti thálassa/ mpalkóni**	tho-ma-tee-o meh the-a stee tha-la-sa/bal-ko-nee
Does the price include breakfast?	**To proïnó symperi-lamvánetai stin timí?**	to pro-ee-no seem-be-ree-lam-va-ne-teh steen tee-mee?

Eating Out

Have you got a table?	**Echete trapézi?**	e-che-te tra-pe-zee?
I want to reserve a table.	**Thélo na kratíso éna trapézi.**	the-lo na kra-tee-so e-na tra-pe-zee.
The bill, please.	**Ton logariazmó parakaló..**	ton lo-gar-yas-mo pa-ra-ka-lo
I am a vegetarian.	**Eímai chortofágos.**	ee-meh chor-to-fa-gos.
What is fresh today?	**Tí frésko échete símera?**	tee fres-ko e-che-teh see-me-ra?
waiter/waitress	**K'yrie/Garson"/ Kyría**	Kee-ree-eh/Gar-son/ Kee-ree-a
menu	**O katálogos**	o ka-ta-lo-gos
cover charge	**To "couvert"**	to koo-ver
wine list	**O katálogos me ta oinopne-vmatódi**	o ka-ta-lo-gos meh ta ee-no-pnev-ma-to-thee
glass	**To potíri**	to po-tee-ree
bottle	**To mpoukáli**	to bou-ka-lee
knife	**To machaíri**	to ma-che-ree
fork	**To piroúni**	to pee-roo-nee
spoon	**To koutáli**	to koo-ta-lee

breakfast	**To proïnó**	to pro-ee-no
lunch	**To mesimerianó**	to me-see-mer-ya-no
dinner	**To deípno**	to theep-no
main course	**To kyríos gévma**	kee-ree-os yev-ma
starter/first course	**Ta orektiká**	ta o-rek-tee-ka
dessert	**To glykó**	to ylee-ko
dish of the day	**To piáto tis i méras**	to pya-to tees ee-me-ras
bar	**To "bar"**	To bar
taverna	**I tavérna**	ee ta-ver-na
café	**To kafeneío**	to ka-fe-nee-o
fish taverna	**I psarotavérna**	ee psa-ro-ta-ver-na
grill house	**I psistariá**	ee psee-sta-rya
wine shop	**To oinopoleío**	to ee-no-po-lee-o
dairy shop	**To galakto-poleío**	to ga-lak-to-po-lee-o
restaurant	**To estiatório**	to e-stee-a-to-ree-o
ouzeri	**To ouzerí**	oo oo-ze-ree
meze shop	**To mezedopoleío**	To me-ze-do-po-lee-o
take away kebabs	**To souvlatzídiko**	To soo-vlat-zee-dee-ko
rare	**Eláchista psiméno**	e-lach-ees-ta psee-me-no
medium	**Métria psiméno**	met-ree-a psee-me-no
well done	**Kalopsiméno**	ka-lo-psee-me-no

Basic Food and Drink

coffee	**O Kafés**	o ka-fes
with milk	**me gála**	me ga-la
black coffee without sugar	**skétos chorís záchari**	ske-tos cho-rees za-cha-ree
medium sweet	**métrios**	me-tree-os
very sweet	**glyk'ys**	glee-kees
tea	**tsái**	tsa-ee
hot chocolate	**zestí sokoláta**	ze-stee so-ko-la-ta
wine	**krasí**	kra-see
red	**kókkino**	ko-kee-no
white	**lefkó**	lef-ko
rosé	**rozé**	ro-ze
raki	**To rakí**	to ra-kee
ouzo	**To oúzo**	to oo-zo

retsina	**I retsína**	ee ret-see-na		100	**ekató**	e-ka-to
water	**To neró**	to ne-ro		200	**diakósia**	thya-kos-ya
octopus	**To chtapódi**	to chta-po-dee		1,000	**chília**	cheel-ya
fish	**To psári**	to psa-ree		2,000	**d'yo chiliádes**	thee-o cheel-ya-thes
cheese	**To tyrí**	to tee-ree		1,000,000	**éna ekatomm'yrio**	e-na e-ka-to-mee-ree-o
halloumi	**To chaloúmi**	to cha-loo-mee		one minute	**éna leptó**	e-na lep-to
feta	**I féta**	ee fe-ta		one hour	**mía óra**	mee-a o-ra
bread	**To psomí**	to pso-mee		half an hour	**misí óra**	mee-see o-ra
bean soup	**I fasoláda**	ee fa-so-la-da		quarter of an hour	**éna tétarto**	e-na te-tar-to
houmous	**To houmous**	to choo-moos		half past one	**mía kai misí**	mee-a keh mee-see
halva	**O chalvás**	o chal-vas		quarter past one	**mía kai tétarto**	mee-a keh te-tar-to
meat kebabs	**O g'yros**	o yee-ros		ten past one	**mía kai déka**	mee-a keh the-ka
Turkish delight	**To loukoúmi**	to loo-koo-mee		quarter to two	**d'yo pará tétarto**	thee-o pa-ra te-tar-to
baklava	**O mpaklavás**	o bak-la-vas		ten to two	**d'yo pará déka**	thee-o pa-ra the-ka
klephtiko	**To kléftiko**	to klef-tee-ko		a day	**mía méra**	mee-a me-ra
				a week	**mía evdomáda**	mee-a ev-tho-ma-tha

Numbers

1	**éna**	e-na		a month	**énas mínas**	e-nas mee-nas
2	**d'yo**	thee-o		a year	**énas chrónos**	e-nas chro-nos
3	**tría**	tree-a		Monday	**Deftéra**	thef-te-ra
4	**téssera**	te-se-ra		Tuesday	**Tríti**	tree-tee
5	**pénte**	pen-deh		Wednesday	**Tetárti**	te-tar-tee
6	**éxi**	ek-si		Thursday	**Pémpti**	pemp-tee
7	**eptá**	ep-ta		Friday	**Paraskeví**	pa-ras-ke-vee
8	**ochtó**	och-to		Saturday	**Sávvato**	sa-va-to
9	**ennéa**	e-ne-a		Sunday	**Kyriakí**	keer-ee-a-kee
10	**déka**	the-ka		January	**Ianouários**	ee-a-noo-a-ree-os
11	**énteka**	en-de-ka		February	**Fevrouários**	fev-roo-a-ree-os
12	**dódeka**	tho-the-ka		March	**Mártios**	mar-tee-os
13	**dekatría**	de-ka-tree-a		April	**Aprílios**	a-pree-lee-os
14	**dekatéssera**	the-ka-tes-se-ra		May	**Máios**	ma-ee-os
15	**dekapénte**	the-ka-pen-de		June	**Ioúnios**	ee-oo-nee-os
16	**dekaéxi**	the-ka-ek-si		July	**Ioúlios**	ee-oo-lee-os
17	**dekaeptá**	the-ka-ep-ta		August	**Avgoustos**	av-goo-stos
18	**dekaochtó**	the-ka-och-to		September	**Septémvrios**	sep-tem-vree-os
19	**dekaennéa**	the-ka-e-ne-a		October	**Októvrios**	ok-to-vree-os
20	**eíkosi**	ee-ko-see		November	**Noémvrios**	no-em-vree-os
21	**eikosiéna**	ee-ko-see-e-na		December	**Dekémvrios**	the-kem-vree-os
30	**triánta**	tree-an-da				
40	**saránta**	sa-ran-da				
50	**penínta**	pe-neen-da				
60	**exínta**	ek-seen-da				
70	**evdomínta**	ev-tho-meen-da				
80	**ogdónta**	og-thon-da				
90	**enenínta**	e-ne-neen-da				

Note: words in bold (centre columns) are transliterated according to the system used by the Greek Government. However, this system is not used consistently throughout Crete, and visitors will encounter many variants on road signs, menus etc.